Groups Interacting With Technology

*Ideas, Evidence,
Issues, and an Agenda*

Joseph E. McGrath
Andrea B. Hollingshead

Sage Library of Social Research 194

SAGE Publications
International Educational and Professional Publisher
Thousand Oaks   London   New Delhi

The research on which this book is based was supported in part by National Science Foundation grant IRI 89-05640 (J. E. McGrath, principal investigator). Reproduction of this material in whole or in part is permitted for any purpose of the United States Government.

For information address:

SAGE Publications, Inc.
2455 Teller Road
Thousand Oaks, California 91320

SAGE Publications Ltd.
6 Bonhill Street
London EC2A 4PU
United Kingdom

SAGE Publications India Pvt. Ltd.
M-32 Market
Greater Kailash I
New Delhi 110 048 India

Printed in the United States of America

Library of Congress Cataloging-in-Publication Data

McGrath, Joseph Edward, 1927-
    Groups interacting with technology : ideas, evidence, issues, and an agenda / authors, Joseph E. McGrath, Andrea B. Hollingshead.
        p. cm. — (Sage library of social research ; 194)
    Includes bibliographical references and indexes.
    ISBN 0-8039-4897-2 (cl.) — ISBN 0-8039-4898-0 (pb)
    1. Work groups—Data processing. 2. Work groups—Data processing—Research. I. Hollingshead, Andrea B. II. Title. III. Series: Sage library of social research ; v. 194.
HD66.M39 1994
658.4'036—dc20   93-34627

94 95 96 97 10 9 8 7 6 5 4 3 2 1

Sage Production Editor: Yvonne Könneker

Contents

Preface

This book resulted from a two-year research project, which was supported by the Information Technology and Organizations program of the Information, Robotics, and Intelligence Division of the National Science Foundation (NSF). The objectives of that project were to review and integrate the burgeoning research literature on the effects of technology on the flow of work in groups, using a group theoretic perspective, and to construct an agenda for future research in that area.

The use of various forms of advanced technology (mostly electronic) to aid the work of groups has spread quite rapidly and widely. There has been a lot written about the wonders—and some about the woes—of such technology. More has been written about what these technologies will do *for* groups than what they will do *to* the groups who use them. There has been a boom in behavioral science research on that topic, or topics closely related to it. But at the time we began this project, the theoretical and empirical research in this area had not been systematically brought together, and its implications for work groups thoroughly plumbed. Furthermore, much of the research dealing with technology did not give much attention to the nature and operation of the groups to which that technology was to be applied, nor to temporal and other aspects of the context within which those applications would occur. Our aim was to carry out a systematic review and assessment of the research literature, giving emphasis simultaneously to the informational, the interactional, and the temporal aspects, as well as to the technological aspects, of those applications of technology.

Successful completion of the project yielded a substantial database—extensive, systematic annotations of more than 250 references. Because the purpose of our work was to make an integrative contribution to research in this area, it seemed appropriate to try to present as full a picture of that body of information as possible, and to as wide an audience of potential users as we could reach. Hence this book. The main body of the book provides a summary and interpretation of the information in that database: the systems used, the guiding conceptual ideas, the body of empirical evidence, and an integration and interpretation of all of it pointing toward future research needs and potential. The appendix of the book presents a condensed summary of the studies that constitute the body of empirical evidence of the field. The bibliography lists all of the relevant literature that we identified.

We had a lot of help from a number of colleagues in carrying out this project, and we want to express our thanks to them. First of all, we thank Dr. Lawrence Rosenberg of the NSF for his faith in our proposed project and for his support of our work. We also thank the many researchers in this field who were extremely generous in supplying us with references, reprints, and preprints of their work, as well as with sound ideas and advice. We especially appreciate a number of researchers who shared their expertise with us in personal interviews and visits to their research facilities: Mark Abel of USWest; Robert Kraut and Carmen Egido of Bellcore; M. Scott Poole, Gerardine DeSanctis, Gary Dickson, and their colleagues at the University of Minnesota; Jay Nunamaker, Doug Vogel, Alan Dennis, Terry Connolly, Joey George, Barbara Gutek, Jolene Galegher, and their colleagues at the University of Arizona; Richard Polley of Lewis and Clark College; Len Jessup of CSUSM; Joe Valacich of Indiana University; Sara Kiesler, Lee Sproull, and their colleagues at Carnegie Mellon University. We are grateful to Scott Poole for his careful and constructive review of an earlier version of this manuscript, and for the helpful comments provided by several anonymous reviewers.

We appreciate the support we got from colleagues at our home university as well. Among those we especially thank are: John Chandler, Noshir Contractor, Karen Gaddis, and Martha Orland. As is the case for many of the things we accomplish, our work on this book was aided immensely by the people who form the social support systems that sustain us, most especially our respective spouses, Marion McGrath and Peter Carnevale.

All of the people named above, and others, have each made contributions that, in different ways, were crucial to our work on this project and this book. We are grateful for their help, and we hope the end product will make a contribution to the field that is worthy of their efforts and our own.

Joseph E. McGrath
Department of Psychology
Andrea B. Hollingshead
Department of Speech Communication
University of Illinois at Urbana-Champaign

Introduction: Electronic Technology in Work Groups

Electronic technologies—especially computers—are ubiquitous in our society. In the workplace, computers are now widely regarded as essential to efficient individual job performance at all levels of organizations—from top management to shop floor, from CEOs to clerical staff. Computers are found in schools and homes, as well as in a wide variety of workplaces. Furthermore, their use has spread very rapidly. As is often the case with rapidly developing technological innovations, the sociocultural systems of the workplace (and schools and homes!) have not entirely adjusted to those technological changes. (Long ago, sociologists coined the term, cultural lag, for just such phenomena.)

Besides the obvious and extensive impact on individual work, computers have also begun to play a large role in the work of groups within organizations. Here, too, the changes have been rapid; and here, too, in many ways, the sociocultural systems have not yet fully "digested" those changes.

Within about a decade computer use has become a part of the everyday lives of a wide range of citizens. Yet they are still regarded by many (including some ardent users) as exotic and mysterious, sometimes miraculous and sometimes malevolent, awesome and awful, panacea and threat.

1

There has, of course, been an outpouring of popular and scholarly literature about computers in the workplace, and about computers as potential technology for collaborative work in groups. Though much of that literature has been speculative expressions of opinion, some of it has contributed important theoretical formulations, and some of it has contained reports of empirical evidence about those systems.

However, much of the theoretical and empirical research regarding uses of computers for collaborative work in groups has been done from the perspective of technology development. Relatively little of it has been done from a group perspective; that is, it has not taken into account the ways in which processes intrinsic to groups affect the ways in which groups adopt, adapt, and use technology. (For an important exception see the work of Poole and colleagues, in Chapter 3 and in the appended annotated bibliography.)

This book is an attempt to shift that balance. One might say that, whereas much past literature has been about *computers in groups*, this book is about *groups with computers*. It is about the use of computers and other electronic technology to aid collaborative work in groups. Our emphasis is on how technology affects the behavior of groups, rather than on the design or functioning of hardware and software systems.

RESEARCH ON GROUPS WITH COMPUTERS

The study of group support systems has been much more about technical developments and applications than about identification and exploration of basic theoretical issues involving the functioning of work groups. Even before the advent of computers and other electronic technology in the area of group support systems, there had been a strong focus on application of specific techniques advocated to improve some aspects of group functioning, and a serious lack of attention to theory, including group theory (again with a few notable exceptions). There has not been much effort given to formulating systematic, integrative conceptual frameworks that would serve as guiding perspectives for future research.

The study of group support systems, like work in most areas of social and behavioral science, has also seriously neglected matters of time (McGrath, 1990; McGrath & Kelly, 1986). There are a myriad of temporal issues central to the work of task groups. These include both issues having to do with the temporal context in which the group's work is being carried out (e.g., deadlines set by agencies outside the group), and issues that have to do with the temporal patterning of the group's behavior (e.g., the synchronization of related acts by different group members).

This lack of attention to groups, to theory, and to time is somewhat ironic considering the early roots of interest in using computers in groups. Efforts to provide groups with technological support have been driven by three basic ideas: improving group task performance, overcoming time and space constraints on group collaborative efforts, and increasing the range and speed of access to information. Those three ideas deserve a closer look.

Improving Task Performance

Much of the early interest in developing systems to support effective performance of various kinds of task groups (e.g., decision-making groups) grew out of group research and theory aimed at increasing group productivity by identifying and eliminating what Steiner (1972) subsequently labeled "process losses." Process losses are those group performance "inefficiencies" (e.g., discussion in the group that is apparently extraneous to the group's assigned task). These are presumably reflected in the extent to which the task performance of a particular group falls short of predictions (derived from the researcher's or practitioner's model) about how the individual efforts and skills of group members would be, could be, or should be combined when those individuals work together as a group on a given type of task.

Efforts to improve group productivity have often taken the form of interventions by which persons managing the situation (group facilitators, researchers, group supervisors) could constrain and structure the communication within the group, the task information available to the group, and/or the form and sequence of task responses permitted and required of the group. Early intervention efforts of this kind are reflected in work identified under labels such as brainstorming (Osborn, 1957; cf. Diehl & Stroebe, 1987,

1991), Delphi method (Dalkey, 1969), nominal group technique (NGT) (e.g., Van de Ven & Delbecq, 1974), multiattribute utility analysis (MAUA) (Eils & John, 1980), and many others. (See McGrath, 1984, for a summary.)

All of the systems used in those earlier decades, however, involved what today might be called "manual" technologies. They did not involve use of electronic or other high-tech devices. Computer-based group support systems are relatively recent developments. These more recent systems, based on electronic technology, raised the sophistication of the (hardware and software) technology of group support systems by several orders of magnitude— but, like the earlier manual systems, they still have not dealt much with groups or with theoretical issues. (For important exceptions, see Poole & DeSanctis, 1990.)

Overcoming Space and Time Constraints

It has long been recognized that groups using electronically enhanced communication systems could transcend the time and space constraints that burden groups who meet face-to-face— namely, that all of their members must be in the same place at the same time in order to meet. There has been some research directly testing the effects of physical separation (as distinct from reduction of communication modalities) on group interaction and task performance. But there has been relatively little work dealing with the possibilities for asynchronous "group meetings," and even less dealing with a myriad of other temporal factors involved in group interaction and performance (with or without electronic technology). (For important exceptions, see work by Kiesler and Sproull and their colleagues; Bikson and colleagues; and Rice and colleagues, in Chapter 3 and in the annotated bibliography.)

Increasing Information Access

It has long been acknowledged that computers could increase the range and depth of information that a given individual (hence, a group), engaged in information-intensive work, could have access to, and also increase the speed and power with which that information could be acquired, processed, presented for use, and shared for collaborative efforts. Even though such enhancement was postulated as a key potential advantage of electronic information systems, research in this area has given little attention to theoretical or conceptual issues about information acquisition, processing, and integration, and even less attention to theoretical issues about the antecedents and consequences of different patterns of information distribution within work groups, and the conditions under which information can be and is easily shared among group members. (For important exceptions, see the work of Malone and colleagues in Chapter 3 and the annotated bibliography.) In this book, we attempt to redress these imbalances regarding groups, theory, and time.

DELINEATING THE DOMAIN OF STUDY

The heart of the effort underlying development of this book was a systematic review, and attempt to integrate, the research literature dealing with the topic of electronic support of collaborative work in groups. That topic—research on the effects of electronic technology on the flow of work in groups—implies at least four major focal concepts to which we gave attention in our review and integration efforts: (a) use of technology, (b) development and functioning of groups, (c) information acquisition and processing in work settings, and (d) temporal issues in individual and group behavior.

There are enormous bodies of work on each one of those four focal concepts, far too much to cover in any single study effort. On the other hand, there is very little work that addresses all four of those focal concepts together, and only a limited amount that addresses any three of them. In between, there are substantial but potentially manageable bodies of work addressing various pairs of those topics. We concentrated our search and integration efforts at that intermediate level, and we gave particular attention to studies involving the first two of those foci—use of technology in groups—whether or not that work dealt explicitly with information processing and/or temporal issues.

ORGANIZATION OF THE BOOK

Chapter 2 ("Systems") lays out a conceptual framework for examining a wide variety of ways in which technology can be used to modify the work of groups and discusses various types of systems within that framework, giving special emphasis to group theoretic issues and to a complex set of temporal issues that those technologies involve. Although we will use the term *technology* broadly in this chapter, most modern means for technological support of work in groups involve electronic systems; at times we will use the term *electronic* interchangeably with *technological*.

In Chapter 3 ("Ideas"), we review the major conceptual ideas that have been employed by a number of different research groups in this domain, noting how some of these ideas are connected to one another. We end that chapter with an attempt to integrate many of the ideas presented in the chapter within our own group theoretic perspective.

Chapter 4 ("Evidence") reviews a large portion of the body of empirical evidence about use of such technologies in work groups, noting both the relatively robust findings and some of the conceptual and methodological limitations of that body of evidence.

In Chapter 5 ("Integration and Agenda"), we attempt to integrate all of the material presented up to that point—about systems, ideas, and evidence—within a group theoretical perspective. We present a conceptual framework that can serve as a guide for systematic research, and then lay out an agenda for future research that will help expand our effective knowledge in this domain.

All of the relevant literature we located is listed in an extensive bibliography in this book. A systematic annotation of the empirical studies we reviewed (see Chapter 4) is presented as an appendix to this book.

T W O

Systems: Applying Electronic Technology in Work Groups

Collaborative work in groups is a complex matter, with or without electronic technology. Collaboration is about more than simply the exchange of information. Collaborative work entails cognitive aspects of communication: Group members transmit, receive, and store information of various kinds, from each other and from various other sources. Collaborative work also entails emotional and motivational aspects of communication: Group members are also transmitting, receiving, and storing the affect and influence aspects of those same messages. Furthermore, these communications may take place within one or another of a number of functionally distinct kinds of communication systems. In principle, each member of a collaborative work group is "hooked up" to four functionally distinct (though not necessarily physically separate), interactive (two-way) communication systems. Those four functionally distinct systems are considered below. Electronic systems for supporting collaborative work in groups also can be classified into these four major categories, on the basis of the functional role that the technology plays in the work of the group. Note, though, that any given operational system may serve more than one of these functions.

I. System(s) for Intragroup Communication

In principle, each member of a collaborative work group can communicate with other members of that group. Each can send information to and receive such information from one or more members of the group. In the ubiquitous small face-to-face group, each member can communicate to all others via a wide spectrum of communication modalities: verbal, paraverbal (e.g., voice inflection), and nonverbal (e.g., smiles and gazes). In other kinds of groups, both the channels (to whom a given member can communicate) and the modalities for communication are often constrained. (These within-group communications, in turn, may become part of a store or log of information dealing with the history and activity of the group; see II, following.)

We can regard human conversation as a series of interlocked communication cycles. Each cycle involves a series of operations on a given message: composition, editing, transmission, reception, feedback (acknowledgment of receipt), and reply. The time to complete such a communication cycle differs for different communication media.

Electronic systems fulfilling this first function, providing or modifying within-group communication, include a variety of systems that have been referred to as group communication support systems, or GCSS. They include video- and audiophones, computer conferences, e-mail, and the like.

II. System(s) for Communication With
Information Bases

In principle, each member of a collaborative work group also is hooked up to a number of bodies of information or knowledge (i.e., databases), beside on-line communication within the group itself (as in I) and on-line communication to individuals outside the group (as in III, following). That is, individual group members can send messages to and/or receive messages from a number of extragroup information stores or databases. Sometimes members can access these databases during the time the group is working collaboratively. In other cases, individuals may have consulted such databases in the recent past and may have direct or indirect access to a repository of that information. These extragroup databases include both quantitative (e.g., sales records, evaluation results, production and cost data) and qualitative (e.g., libraries, newspaper files) bodies of information. They also include historical information stores or archives—at least in memory—that contain representations of events from the member's own history, and from the history of the group and its embedding organization. Obviously, different members of the group have direct individual access to different arrays of possible sources of information, some of them directly available (in unprocessed form) only to that member. Hence, in the general case, potentially relevant information should be regarded as a valuable and inevitably distributed resource that can be, but may not be, shared within a given group.

Electronic systems serving this second function—supplementing information available to the group or its members by information drawn from data stores—include systems both for accessing information from databases and other information archives, and for selecting, processing, and presenting that information.

III. System(s) for External Communication

At the same time (in principle) each member of a collaborative work group can communicate with a number of individuals and groups outside the current work group—for example, colleagues, supervisors, content experts, teachers, and sometimes even family and friends. Sometimes such communication channels are arbitrarily curtailed (by normative agreement or by physical arrangements) during all or portions of the collaborative activities (e.g., "Hold my calls during this meeting" and "Please don't call me at the office"), with such extragroup communications taking place before and during recesses in collaborative group activity. But sometimes those extragroup communications are vital to the group's progress and success; for example, communications to and from the group's direct supervisor, or communications to get timely information about availability of vital resources.

Electronic systems that serve the third function—providing or modifying communication between the group or its members and key agencies outside the group—are, for the most part, parallel to the varieties of systems used for internal group communication, and are more or less a special case of such Group Communication Support Systems (GCSS) that serve a different function for the group.

IV. System(s) for Structuring Group Task Performance

Finally, in principle, each group member needs to be able to receive task information and perform task activities; that is, each member needs to be in two-way communication with relevant tasks. Just as systems for communicating among group members (see I, earlier) structure the form, content, and flow of those messages, systems for channeling task inputs and responses structure both the nature of the task activities of members and the nature of the task products resulting from those activities. A group member's task activities may or may not be done interdependently, or in parallel, with task activities of other members of the group. Different group members may do different tasks in pursuit of a common group goal.

Electronic systems serving the fourth function—channeling or modifying the group's task performance processes and task products—include a variety of tools that structure the form in which tasks are presented to the group and the form of the group's potential task responses. The modules often used in group decision support systems to structure idea generation, idea evaluation, agenda setting, and so forth, are cases in point (see later discussion).

To parallel the terminology current in the field, but yet adapt it to our particular classification system, we will call these four categories, respectively:

   I. GCSS: Group (Internal) Communication Support Systems
   II. GISS: Group Information Support Systems
   III. GXSS: Group External Communication Support Systems
   IV. GPSS: Group Performance Support Systems

Often, these types of systems are intermeshed in practice. It is nevertheless useful to keep them distinguished for purposes of discussion and analysis. This is especially the case in regard to temporal issues; the technological systems in each of these categories involve a number of crucial, but different, temporal issues, many of which have been largely overlooked in research to date.

The four sections of this chapter identify and examine important features for each of the four categories of group support systems, especially those that have impact on crucial group and temporal issues. Before discussing features of those systems in detail, we want to insert caveats about our coverage and our purposes. First, we consider the various systems (for example, audio communication systems such as telephones and text communication systems such as computer conferences) when such a system is used separately; we do not discuss those systems used in combination. Furthermore, we consider only systems that have been used, studied, and reported on in forms to which we could get access. Hence we do not consider a lot of cutting edge developments, nor do we take into account probable near-future developments in this rapidly developing field. Our purpose is not to assess all of the technological possibilities, currently and in the near future; rather, it is to consider the effects of various features of technological systems on aspects of group process and performance. We expect any given technological system to lead to both advantageous and disadvantageous features of group process and performance. It is not only possible, but indeed very likely, that in the future, by combinations of current systems, and/or by introduction of radically new systems, advanced technological systems will be attained with features that overcome or offset some of the disadvantages and enhance some of the advantages found when current systems are considered separately.

GCSS: TECHNOLOGIES THAT MODIFY THE GROUP'S INTERNAL COMMUNICATION SYSTEM

Electronic systems that facilitate communication within work groups have been called, collectively, group communication support systems (GCSS), electronic meeting systems (EMS), and similar labels (Dennis, George, Jessup, Nunamaker, & Vogel, 1988;

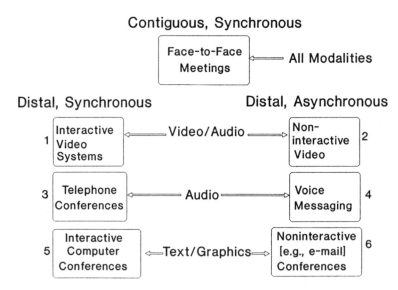

Figure 2.1. Six Types of GCSS
SOURCE: Adapted from McGrath and Hollingshead (1993).

DeSanctis & Gallupe, 1987; Kraemer & King, 1988). These offer one major benefit and one major cost. On the positive side, various types of electronic communication permit group members to "meet," functionally though not physically, even when they are physically dispersed and operating at different times. On the other hand, various types of electronic communication reduce the set of modalities by which group members can communicate with one another. Various channels—auditory, visual, nonverbal, paraverbal, and so on—are precluded. The extent of that reduction of modalities depends on the particular GCSS used. The importance of that reduction of modalities (and, indeed, whether it is a cost or a benefit, according to some proponents) depends on the particular task(s) and activities in which the group is engaged (McGrath & Hollingshead, 1993).

Figure 2.1 shows six major types of GCSS, classified with regard to some of their main distinguishing features. The ubiquitous, non-technologically enhanced type—ordinary face-to-face communication—is also shown in that figure, to place the GCSS in an appropriate comparative context.

In Figure 2.1, GCSS are classified along two axes:

1. the requirements they impose (and the opportunities they permit) regarding spatial and temporal distribution of group members; and
2. the modalities they provide (and those they preclude) for within-group communication among group members.

In contrast to face-to-face systems, all six types of GCSS permit (but do not require) group members to be spatially separated from each other—in different buildings, different cities, different countries, or merely in different rooms—while they are communicating. Three of those types permit (but do not require) group members to be acting in different time periods (asynchronously); the other three require that group members interact synchronously (as do face-to-face systems).

Two of the types use visual and auditory modalities; these can embed text and graphics, but in noninteractive forms. Two of the types use an auditory but not a visual modality; these have no text or graphics. Two of the types permit only text and graphics.

Synchronous Video Systems

Three types of synchronous video systems—video walls, video-conferencing, and videophones—provide the means for auditory and visual interaction among group members who are spatially dispersed but acting in temporal synchrony. When first envisioned, such video systems seemed to offer great promise as convenient and low-cost alternatives to face-to-face meetings for groups whose members were geographically separated. The reality has proven less spectacular than the promise (Abel, 1990; Egido, 1990; Kraut, Fish, Root, & Chalfonte, 1990).

Video Walls

The first type of synchronous video systems, video walls or video windows, provides continuous, interactive audio/video connections between fixed locations (a "commons" area) in each of two sites. With the system always "on," there is more or less automatic audio/video communication between any individuals who enter those commons areas. There have been at least two major design efforts to provide such continuous, two-way, interactive video/audio connections between groups in two locations (Abel, 1990; Goodman & Abel, 1987; Kraut, Fish, Root, & Chalfonte, 1990). For both of those efforts, the aim seems to have been to provide people working in distant locations with an approximation of the kind of continuous, low-effort, full modality access that people have to one another when they work in the same office area.

Videoconferences

Videoconferences provide video/audio connections between people in two (or more) spatially dispersed locations, at a specific time (rather than continuously), usually with the camera in each site controllable from the other site. Videoconferencing has been touted as the prototype for the meeting of the future—a close approximation of face-to-face conditions that would greatly reduce travel costs.

Videophones

The videophone links one individual with a second, specifically targeted person, in both video and audio channels. This might be regarded as the limiting, two-person case of a videoconference.

All three of these types of systems have been heralded optimistically but have had meager success when used as a basis for collaborative group work. Even though these systems provide relatively broadband communication, in auditory and visual modalities, that communication often is seriously degraded. The quality of both auditory and visual transmission, and the integration of the two, has proven problematic thus far in both video walls and videoconferences (Abel, 1990; Abel, Corey, Bulick, Schmidt, & Coffin, 1992; Egido, 1990; Kraut, Fish, Root, & Chalfonte, 1990). These authors expect that as technology improves, the auditory and visual quality problems will diminish.

All of the systems in this category require communication that is synchronous in time (that is, all parties are acting at the same time, although in different places). They give rise to at least two sets of temporal issues:

1. These systems apparently created some problems in regulation of the flow of communication between the two facilities (Abel, 1990). They carry considerable visual information, but they apparently do not carry as much nonverbal "back-channel" information as face-to-face communication does. Absence of such back-channel information can hinder smooth transitions between speakers located at different, distant sites.

2. If the sites are very distant, there are likely to be some time lags in transmission and feedback, and these may be different for visual and auditory channels. Electronic transmission is rapid, but not instantaneous in any modality. Although human interaction is not attuned to a nanosecond level, it is sensitive to intervals of about 100 milliseconds or more.

The visual modality in these systems permits transmission of material in written form. Charts in one room can be seen in another. But presentation is often much less interactive than it would be in a face-to-face situation. For technologies used to date, people in one facility cannot directly alter written material in the other site. However, various methods have been proposed for using "electronic chalk boards" and other technologies generally referred to as "hypermedia" (Landow, 1990; Yankelovich, Haan, Meyrowitz, & Drucker, 1988); such recent technological developments may eliminate that limitation on interactivity. The rapid spread of relatively low-cost fax capabilities suggests another indirect route to achieve interactivity with regard to text and graphics at distant sites.

Most of the research reports about the strengths and weaknesses of those systems provide only anecdotal reports of a particular use of a particular system, rather than systematic evidence about repeated (or extensive) testing with different user groups. This is in part because development and application of such systems, even on a single case basis, are very costly in time, money, and other resources. A thorough assessment of these systems will not be possible until more systematic evaluation studies have been done.

Noninteractive (Asynchronous)
Video Systems

Asynchronous forms of GCSS, parallel to the video systems just discussed, make use of video technology but do so in ways that do not permit synchronous or interactive communication. Included here, for example, would be the use of videotapes or laser disks, transmitted from a "source" to a "target," to be viewed at a time of convenience for the target. In such uses, the videotapes could either be recorded at the source and shipped, or transmitted electronically and recorded at the destination for later presentation.

For example: Imagine that a scheduled speaker, unable to attend a conference, prerecorded the talk that was then "given" via videocassette. The audience's reaction to the talk, including posttalk discussion, could in turn be videotaped and sent back to the speaker.

Both temporal and qualitative issues can be raised about such communications. Experientially, the "full-band" video and audio presentation would probably seem much richer to the audience than an audio-only presentation (or a written-text only presentation) would have been. But it would still be distinctly noninteractive, compared with what even a very formal presentation to a large audience would have been. It certainly would have a distinctly different quality vis-à-vis the speaker's "presence" than a live presentation would have had. For example, the audience would be acutely aware that they could not ask the speaker any questions (and that the speaker would not in any way react to anything that happened while the talk was being "given").

For video systems, the asynchronous case imposes a strong temporal burden on communication. There are substantial time lags between composition, transmission, and reception, and still longer ones between those stages and feedback. These time lags are discussed later under computer conference systems (synchronous and asynchronous), because they impose even more of a temporal burden there. If the information required rapid updating in terms of current status, this kind of GCSS would be wholly inadequate.

Telephone Conferences

This type of synchronous GCSS is relatively familiar; in the two-party case it is the ultrafamiliar phone call. There has been considerable research on such systems, much of it well summarized by Williams (1977). These systems use only the auditory modality, eliminating not only the cues that go with physical presence (as for video, above), but also all cues in the visual modality (e.g., nonverbal behavior; information in written form). It does, however, preserve important paraverbal aspects of speech. Nonverbal behavior expressed through the visual modality (e.g., facial expressions, nods, direction of gaze) is very important as a back-channel for feedback in interacting groups. Its loss often creates serious problems for the group in managing the temporal patterning of the group's communication; that is, the flow of speakers, pauses, interruptions, and so on. There may be substantial transmission time lags for telephone conferences involving very long (e.g., intercontinental) distances—lags far longer than 100 milliseconds (the level to which humans are sensitive). These can disrupt the smooth flow of conversation.

Voice Messaging

The asynchronous GCSS that parallel telephone conferences in Figure 2.1 are voice messaging systems, some of which provide elaborate technology of the familiar telephone answering systems (Rice & Shook, 1990b). These are like telephone conferences in that they rely entirely on communication in the auditory mode, with the advantages and disadvantages that accompany that modality (see above). They differ from telephone conferences in that they are not interactive. Thus participant A must compose and send a complete message, then wait for participant B to receive it and respond, in order to get any feedback about the first message. B cannot give interactive feedback to A in the course of A's composition and transmission of the initial first message, as B readily could do in face-to-face groups and, to some degree, in synchronous telephone conversations. As for all asynchronous systems, however, these systems complicate the sequencing of sent and received messages, especially when three or more parties are involved.

One of the strengths of voice messaging is its presentation of paraverbal cues that can aid the expression of emotion and the interpretation of subtle meanings. These are extremely valuable in face-to-face communication, and totally missing in computer-mediated communications (see below). The importance of these cues for effective communication is discussed under synchronous and asynchronous computer conferences, because the loss of such paraverbal cues represent serious disadvantages for communication in those systems.

Synchronous Computer Conferences

These systems permit communication among group members only via computer, hence permit interactive transmission only of written text and graphics. This type of system imposes all of the modality restrictions established by the types of systems discussed previously—video systems and telephone conferences—and some additional ones as well. In computer conferences, all nontext visual and auditory information is eliminated, and with them all nonverbal and paraverbal cues. (Note that these comments reflect the current status of computer conference systems that are widely available. It is clear that in the near future, technology that combines text, audio, and visual information with at least some degree of two-way interactivity will be available for computer conferences.)

Nonverbal and paraverbal cues serve at least three important functions in group communication: They help regulate the flow of communication; they express emotion; and they transmit subtle meanings. Regarding the regulatory function: Paraverbal and nonverbal cues help group members regulate succession of speakers, timing of turn taking, and the like. Consequently, there is an increase in the turbulence of the flow of communications when paraverbal and nonverbal modalities are eliminated from interaction. Regarding the emotive function: The vital role that paraverbal cues play in interpretation of subtle meanings in spoken speech can be partly replaced in written speech by use of a variety of techniques. These include (a) longer and more complex syntax; (b) jargon, argot, and other shared nonstandard language that relies on culturally shared connotative meanings; (c) punctuation and format conventions; and (d) redundancy. These provide, at best, a low-quality substitute for what humans routinely do with paraverbal and nonverbal cues. Some have tried to replace the expressive function of paraverbal cues by use of special symbols and conventions in computer-generated text. These are sometimes referred to as "emoticons." These, too, are low-quality and time costly practices compared to what humans can do elegantly (and eloquently) with the nonsemantic aspects of speech.

Four aspects of the temporal patterning of work differ between such computer-aided groups and face-to-face groups:

1. Production: Most people can talk much faster than even very skilled typists can type.
2. Reception: Most people can read faster than they listen, although the amount of that difference depends on type of material (e.g., complex mathematical formulas are likely to be much harder to hear than to see), skill of the listener/reader, speed of presentation by the speaker, and number and intensity of competing stimuli in the same modality.
3. Transmission: For computer-mediated communication, composition, editing, and transmission of a message are often separate operations, done sequentially. The editing step takes time but can improve the quality of the message. In the face-to-face case, composition, editing, and transmission are all on-line and simultaneous. Eliminating the editing step may save time, but does not allow for correction of slips of the tongue.
4. Simultaneous composition: In computer conferences, more than one member can (and usually does) compose and send messages at the same time. In face-to-face groups, however, there is almost always only one speaker at a time (McGrath, 1990). Thus there is less "production blocking" (Diehl & Stroebe, 1991; Lamm & Trommsdorff, 1973)—that is, less competition for floor time—in computer conferences. Simultaneously, there is a potentially high cost in cognitive load: n members are generating messages for each member to read.

These, in turn, pose a number of potential temporal problems in the flow of messages among members. For example: If composition takes different amounts of time for different members, and transmission takes some additional finite time, then not only is receipt of a message separated in time from its composition, but messages also may be received and sent in different sequences by different participants. Furthermore, because multiple sources can transmit at the same time, the reading load is likely to increase rapidly with small increases in group size. There may be a certain group size above which the elimination of production blocking becomes a negative, not a positive, feature.

Asynchronous Computer Conferences

Asynchronous computer conference systems are sometimes called electronic bulletin board (EBB) and electronic mail (e-mail) systems. They have proliferated enormously in recent years.

When group members are dispersed in both space and time, several temporal issues enter directly: The sequencing of messages, the orderly flow of communication, and the time required for a communication cycle are all potentially affected. In face-to-face conversation, all members receive messages in the same order; and the temporal patterning of the actions of different members typically becomes "entrained" (Kelly, Futoran, & McGrath, 1990; McGrath & Kelly, 1986) to each other, producing a smooth and synchronized flow of conversation most of the time (e.g., smooth transitions among speakers, few long silences, few interruptions). In asynchronous computer conferences, the natural order of messages is potentially disrupted—different participants are likely to receive and respond to messages in different sequences—and so is the smooth, synchronized flow of conversation.

For example: Members A and B might compose and send messages to the group at different times. Members C and D each might read those two messages back-to-back, but at different times from one another. In fact, member C might read and respond to the messages from A and B, and A and B might both reply to C, before member D reads the initial messages from A and B. In such a case, when member D eventually begins to read these messages, he or she would enter in the middle of a full-blown "conversation" and could only participate in its later stages.

GCSS often alter communication times, as well as the sequence and synchrony of messages. For electronic communication systems, the flow of a given communication cycle entails a finite (although relatively short) transmission time, a fairly substantial composition time (because typing is slower than talking), and perhaps an extensive editing time. In asynchronous computer communication systems, there may be no automatic feedback about the reception of a message, and there may be no unambiguous cues regarding acknowledgment and feedback; such cues are usually available for face-to-face communication or for synchronous computer, video, and telephone communications. Hence there is no direct means for a sender to know that his or her message has been received by (as distinct from delivered to) any particular potential receiver.

Media differ, moreover, in the size, nature, and ambiguity of the set of interactive partners. In synchronous computer conferences, the set of interactive partners is likely to be relatively small and that set is by definition a closed set. Under those conditions, people may operate on the assumption that members receive messages more or less immediately. Hence failure of a given member to reply in a timely fashion can be regarded as a deliberate choice by that member, because it is assumed by other members that the member in question has received, read, and chosen not to respond to the message. This same assumption is ordinarily made in face-to-face groups, and it can be verified by nonverbal and auditory channels (e.g., nonverbal feedback via smiles, gazes, head nods, and the like). In asynchronous computer conferences, however, the set of potential receivers is likely to be large, and in any case it is an open set and may be unknown to a sender. So the assumption that all potential receivers have in fact read and understood a given message within a short span of time is not likely to be warranted. Hence ambiguity is increased in an asynchronous computer conference, because the sender cannot be confident that failure of any given member to reply to a given message in a timely fashion reflects that member's deliberate choice.

A Concluding Comment

Earlier, we inserted a caveat: That we are not examining all possible combinations of these technological support systems, nor are we examining radically new systems now in development. For completeness, we should note here that fax systems provide a relatively new electronic technology for text and graphics exchange in collaborative work. There have long been nonelectronic systems for such exchanges: letters, memos, reports, and the like; but in the past such print media have been limited to the asynchronous case for physically separate groups. (They can be used synchronously for groups in spatial proximity.) Fax permits such near-synchronous exchange of text and graphics material for physically separate groups as well. When fax is considered as a separate system, it represents a variant of the asynchronous computer conference, one with relatively low interactivity. But when fax is considered in combination with other systems—for example, in combination with video and audio conferences—it can add considerable potential for interactive exchange of text and graphics material.

Concluding Comments About GCSS

These six types of GCSS differ in the advantages and limitations they bring to the group's internal communication. In general, successive restriction of modalities constrains the amount and the richness of information that can be transmitted. Such restriction can be a boon or a bane for the group, depending on the circumstances. These modality restrictions are an inevitable consequence of using systems that permit groups to overcome spatial and temporal dispersion. Freeing groups from these spatial and temporal constraints, like modality restrictions, brings a mix of good news and bad news from the point of view of making work groups effective.

Of course, GCSS are only part of the story. Group support systems that perform three other functions are the topic of subsequent sections of the chapter.

GISS: TECHNOLOGIES THAT MODIFY
THE GROUP'S INFORMATION BASE

All individuals have access to many bodies of information or knowledge from sources other than on-line communication with interaction partners. At the very least, all members have, in the recent past, sent and received messages from a number of extragroup information sources, and still have at least some representation of those communications available (in memory or elsewhere). These extragroup sources include quantitative databases, such as sales records and production and cost data, and qualitative databases or archives, such as information stored in libraries and newspaper files. They also include information stores or archives that contain representations of events from the individual's or group's own histories—both formal archives, like the minutes of the previous meeting, and informal ones, like memories of the sharp disagreement between Peggy and George in last week's staff meeting.

When people work in a collaborative group, some of the databases to which they have access may contain knowledge useful for that group performance context. Different members of a given group will have direct access to different arrays of possible sources of information. For some of those bodies of information (e.g., one's own past history, present intentions, and future plans and expectations) there is only one individual who can have direct access. Thus no individual can have direct access to all possible information sources. But if the group has a GCSS—indeed, if the group can meet in any sense—then, in principle, every group member has indirect access to all of the information sources that any one member can reach. (That is, the group's potential information is the union of all of the information accessible to each of the members.) The extent to which group members fully share all information available to them, however, is always problematic, and is a matter of considerable consequence for effective group performance. (That is, the group's actual common information is the intersect, not the union, of the information available to the members.)

It always costs, in time and effort, to acquire, store, and retrieve information from any source, and there is an additional cost to disseminate it to others. Hence information can be regarded as a resource that is (a) potentially scarce (that is, not everyone has all of it at the outset), (b) potentially valuable (that is, it may be useful for self or others to have it), and (c) potentially costly to obtain and to share. In any given case, some information possessed by individual group members will be disseminated to others (both intentionally and unintentionally), and some will not.

All of this holds for GISS with or without electronic technology. As noted earlier, one of the main potential advantages of the use of computers in information-intensive work has been the obvious potential for increasing the range and depth of information that a given individual (or group) could have access to, and for increasing the speed and power with which that information can be acquired, processed, and presented for use.

The speed and power with which electronic technology can handle information has grown even greater, along with the feasibility of providing such GISS capability to one or more members of any given group. Clearly, the problem is no longer one of insuring that group members can have access to enough extant information. Rather, the key problems in this domain have to do with information integration and overload, on one hand, and information distribution and sharing on the other.

Integration and Overload

Modern electronic media can acquire, process, and present information with such speed and power that groups with electronic GISS will continually be on the verge of disastrous information overload unless some active measures are taken to fend it off. There is an irony here: For members not to share information crucial to the group's tasks will hurt group productivity. At the same time, for members to share all the information they have with all other group members could have even more disastrous consequences. A single group member connected to electronically accessible bodies of information can pump in enough information to overwhelm the human information-processing capabilities of the entire group, unless those processing capabilities are also enhanced by some powerful technological means. It is important, therefore, that techniques be developed to provide efficient and effective integrations of important task information, and efficient and effective forms in which filtered and focused information transmission among group members can take place. It is also important to explore issues involved in the distribution and sharing of information in collaborative work groups.

Part of the promise of electronic technology has always been its capacity to manage as well as to acquire information. For at least half a century, computers have been looked on as the method of choice to provide means for filtering, processing, and integrating information, as well as for acquiring it. Such information processing and integrating is a major function served by the fourth type of group support system (GPSS), to be discussed later. But even with the best of information management systems, it is still the case that current technology for information gathering and storing is so powerful that information overload is a serious and continuing potential problem for any work group.

Overload is clearly a temporal issue. Load is always reckoned with respect to some group's (or other system's) processing capacity during some period of time. Overloads come in two forms, from a temporal point of view. In one form, the tasks themselves are time-urgent; they must be done within a certain limited time period or not at all. Intercepting a missile (or five of them simultaneously in flight) would be a case in point. In such circumstances, task overload translates into a matter of speed of response. In the other form, overload simply refers to having too many things to do at once, or too many stimuli to attend to at once, even though the tasks themselves do not have a critical time component. That kind of overload can be translated into a matter of priority and sequence of tasks, provided the operating system is expanded in capacity or given a longer period of time to complete the total set of tasks. Information overload is a potentially serious problem for groups with electronic GISS. These temporal features of task overload, as well as the information-processing features, should be given more research attention than has been the case to date.

Information Distribution and Sharing

For the most part, information acquisition and processing takes place at the individual level. Any one or more members of the group may bring information of a particular kind from a particular source into the group via some form of GISS (or GXSS; see next section). If that information is to become a group resource or part of a group product, it must be disseminated, essentially through the group's GCSS. The conditions under which information held by an individual member is or is not shared in the group represents an important area that researchers have just begun to explore (for a summary, see Stasser & Stewart, 1992).

But a piece of information does not have to be shared to have an impact on group process and outcome. For example, a group leader might have access to information about particular goals that management wishes the group to maximize in its work (e.g., keeping travel and other short-run costs down until the end of the fiscal year; reducing dependence on a particular supplier). The leader might choose not to tell the group about those priorities, but that knowledge about priorities is nevertheless likely to affect the leader's interaction, and thereby affect the group's resultant product.

This poses a dilemma regarding the sharing of information for any work group that must stay in business for even a moderate length of time. It is a problem at the interface of GISS and GCSS, rather than within either one. On one hand, the more the group's activity is being affected by closely held information, with each member's interaction being channeled by information available only to that member, the more the individual group members are likely to feel (correctly!) that the others have hidden agendas and are manipulating the group. This feeling, in turn, is likely to engender mutual distrust and suspicion among group members; such groups will probably find it progressively harder to attain consensus and group members may find it harder to work harmoniously and effectively as a group.

This discussion points to an extremely important set of issues, far too complex for adequate treatment here: the question of individual privacy and threats to privacy that electronic technology makes possible. One special form of that problem is the case of information that one member holds in confidence. Sometimes individual group members have information (because of their roles outside the particular group) that cannot legitimately be shared with all members of that group. Yet, if known to one member, it can (and often should) affect that member's activities whether intended or not (as discussed in the previous example). To share that information with others in the group is to violate its confidentiality. But if the information is not shared, yet its existence is mentioned by the person who claims to have access to such information ("I can't tell you about it, but I have reason to believe that . . ."), that can be seen by others as an influence tactic on the part of the putative "knower," and some of the same problems of intermember trust can arise.

On the other hand, the more the individual members of the group choose to share (via GCSS) the information available to each of them, the more likely it is that all group members will suffer from serious information overload, or else will begin ignoring the information they get from others, or both. How big these effects are, and how rapidly they come about, will depend on the group's task, as well as its own composition and history. But as information continues to increase, some overload effects are virtually inevitable. Overloaded groups will find it progressively more difficult to carry out any segment of their tasks, including achieving consensus. In the longer run, they too may have problems of intragroup harmony and trust.

Various methods for filtering and processing information and for reducing and/or simplifying the information as actually presented, have been developed as means for dealing with potential information overload. These tend to be quite specific to the particular body of information involved. The methods can be very effective, provided they screen out or reorganize information in ways that maximize the ends-in-view of that particular group. But such systems also can screen out (and/or otherwise distort) information that member(s) of a particular group want or need. The information filtering and processing system (or its designer) becomes the arbiter of what information the group should/can have and in what form. That, too, is a potential problem of substantial magnitude as information systems become more complex.

These issues apply to the acquisition and use of information in groups with or without electronic technology. The enormous extension of speed and power of access to information that electronic systems bring increases the impact of all of these issues manyfold.

GXSS: TECHNOLOGIES THAT MODIFY THE GROUP'S EXTERNAL COMMUNICATION SYSTEM

A third major function that electronic technology can serve for work groups is to provide a system to support their communication with key agents external to the group. In a sense, this function is a special case of both the GCSS function and the GISS function, previously discussed. In general, the six types of support systems already described under GCSS are applicable to GXSS as well. Communications between the group (or its members) and key agents external to it can be done with systems using any of the three combinations of modalities (video, audio, text/graphics), and any of the patterns of spatial and temporal distribution (e.g., temporally synchronous and spatially proximal; temporally synchronous but spatially dispersed; temporally asynchronous and spatially dispersed) described for the GCSS systems. Consequently, much of what has already been said about the six types of GCSS applies, as well, to the group's external communication system. At the same time, one can consider interaction with individuals outside the group as accessing another kind of information database, thus a special case of GISS as well. In that regard, the problems of potential overload, information distribution, and information sharing, and of differential member access to information crucial to the group's work, discussed earlier, are applicable here.

External communication by groups and group members, to individuals and groups outside the referent work group, has been given much less attention in the research literature than has internal group communication—not just in regard to electronically mediated systems, but in the general literature on group theory and research. Ancona and her colleagues (Ancona & Caldwell, 1988, 1990) have pioneered research showing that external relations, including external communications, is vital to effective leadership and to group success in certain kinds of knowledge-intensive work groups. There has been little other published work dealing with this external communication function. This is an area in which further research is clearly needed.

GPSS: TECHNOLOGIES THAT MODIFY THE GROUP'S PERFORMANCE PROCESSES

As noted earlier, the idea of group support systems existed before the advent of computers, or at least before their use in such capacities. Since before midcentury, practitioners have been trying to devise ways to improve group effectiveness, and specifically to help groups avoid what Steiner (1972) subsequently called *process losses*.

All of the systems used in those earlier decades, however, involved what we might call in the present context manual technologies. They did not involve use of electronic or other high-tech devices. Computer-based group decision support systems, and so-called decision rooms, are relatively recent developments. Two facilities have pioneered those developments:

1. GroupSystems developed by Nunamaker and his colleagues at the University of Arizona (Dennis et al., 1988; Vogel & Nunamaker, 1990; Vogel, Nunamaker, George, & Dennis, 1988). GroupSystems is a DOS-based system (or set of systems) designed for use with relatively larger groups (eight or more members) and with a facilitator. It is now marketed by the Ventana Corporation of Tucson, Arizona.

2. The Software Assisted Meeting Management (SAMM) system, and its descendants, developed by DeSanctis, Dickson, Poole, and their colleagues at the University of Minnesota (DeSanctis & Poole, 1990; Poole, 1991; Poole & DeSanctis, 1990). SAMM is a unix-based system (or set of systems) designed for use with relatively smaller groups (four to eight members).

These two systems, and their progeny, have dominated research in this area for the past decade. They are quite distinct systems, developed along different lines, using different hardware and software, and reflecting the somewhat different purposes of their protagonists. Both attempt to provide (electronic) tools to support, and presumably to improve, task performance of groups.

In recent years, a number of other task performance support systems, many direct or indirect descendants of GroupSystems and SAMM, have been developed. (See Jessup & Valacich, 1993, for discussions of many of them.) Electronic systems that provide direct task performance support for groups usually incorporate an array of modules, each of which structures a different subset of a group's tasks—or, to borrow terms from prior work (McGrath, 1990, 1991), to structure different portions of the group's production function on a given project. A typical system might include a list of tools or modules such as the following (adapted from Nunamaker, Vogel, & Konsynski, 1989):

a module to help manage the system;
a module for electronic brainstorming;
an issue analyzer module;
a module to structure various forms of evaluation and voting (rating, ranking, weights, pick one, pick any, etc.);
a module to aid in policy formation;
a module to facilitate identifying stakeholders and bringing their assumptions to the surface;
a module to aid in examining organizational (or group) infrastructure (see GISS); and
a module that permits exchange of comments on any or all topics (that is, that provides more or less unstructured communication within the group via text/graphics; see GCSS).

Different systems (and, indeed, different presentations of the same system) include somewhat differing lists. One major characteristic of all of these GPSS systems is that they remain continually under development; their developers and users continually generate new modules that expand the scope and comprehensiveness of group activities to which those systems are directed.

Such continual growth, although bespeaking the vitality of the problem area and of the development efforts, also bespeaks a kind of conceptual chaos that besets the area. The rapid growth in number and capabilities of such systems has been done largely without conceptual guidance. Early on, the development of new modules was driven mainly by technological feasibility, which becomes less and less problematic as programming, software, and hardware advances come into play. Many modules have been developed to fit local interests in technological support of specific existing manual group procedures (e.g., a stakeholder analysis, a brainstorming procedure). More recently, there has been some effort given to a conceptual analysis of the likely importance of various kinds of potential modules to specific substantive systems that are the intended beneficiaries of these developments (e.g., What do spatially dispersed decision-making groups need? What will aid coauthors trying to write a report from separate sites?). Such efforts require a prior theoretical analysis of the functioning of such groups and, on a more general scale, would require a general theory of groups within which to conduct such an analysis. This is an area in which the lack of interest in theoretical considerations, noted earlier in the book, has limited systematic development.

These GPSS systems presume that most work groups need help in performing some or all of their task activities, such as setting an agenda, identifying problems, generating alternatives, choosing among alternatives, negotiating consensus with one another, and so on. They provide a set of modules that the group can (sometimes, that the group must) call on to do these tasks. Each module is designed to help structure activities pertaining to a certain type of task.

These systems are intended to improve both speed and quality of group productivity. There have been remarkably broad claims about such improvements in the published literature. In our view, the empirical support regarding such claims is quite equivocal and controversial. That evidence will be examined in some detail in Chapter 4. We take issue, as well, with the underlying idea that differences in task performance speed, or apparent efficiency, should automatically be regarded (pejoratively) as process losses. That set of issues will be discussed, in the context of our group theoretical integration, in Chapters 3 and 5. We turn now, in Chapter 3, to consideration of some of the guiding ideas that underlie the development, use, and evaluations of these systems.

THREE

Ideas: Major Conceptual Formulations About the Effects of Electronic Technology in Work Groups

As noted earlier, much of the impetus for development of technological support for work groups has been motivated by one or more of three underlying assumptions:

1. Improving task performance of work groups: One key assumption has been that technologically enhanced support systems could be built to improve group task performance effectiveness, thereby helping groups overcome so-called process losses by altering group task performance processes.
2. Overcoming space and time constraints on groups: Another important assumption has been that electronic technology could literally redefine the temporal and spatial prerequisites for group work—namely, that all group members must be in the same place at the same time in order to meet—by permitting extensive, rapid, and interactive communication among individuals who were spatially and temporally dispersed, thereby creating groups that would not have been possible heretofore.
3. Increasing access to information: A third key assumption has been that technology (notably computers) could increase the range and depth of information to which a given individual (or group), engaged in information-intensive work, has access; and could increase the speed and power with which such information could be acquired, processed, and used.

This chapter presents some of the ideas of 17 groups of re-searchers whose work, collectively, makes up a very large portion of the conceptual foundations of this area of study. Here, we con-centrate on their conceptual contributions. Empirical contributions are reviewed in Chapter 4.

Our presentation is organized partly in terms of the three as-sumptions above, partly in terms of the four functions of technol-ogy that were presented in Chapter 2 (GPSS, GCSS, GISS, and GXSS), and partly in chronological terms. We begin by discussing the conceptual formulations of two research groups whose work focuses on the first assumption, using technology to structure and support group meetings in order to improve group task perform-ance. These are concerned with systems of the type we called GPSS in Chapter 2. Next we discuss the conceptual contributions of four research groups that focus on the second assumption, using tech-nology to modify communication networks and patterns of rela-tionships within organizations—in effect, to modify the nature of work and of work relationships. These give attention to systems we called GCSS in Chapter 2.

The third section of the chapter covers contributions of several sets of researchers whose work has focused on the study of tem-poral, informational, and interactive processes in work groups, and in doing so have focused on the GISS and GXSS functions—although they have not necessarily dealt with groups using elec-tronic technology. We think their work contains part of the in-tellectual foundation for the topic area with which we are dealing, and that it can provide valuable insights into potential effects of technology on those temporal, informational, and interactive pro-cesses in work groups.

The fourth section deals with conceptions that focus not on work groups but on the organizational contexts within which those groups are embedded. They are concerned with both the second and third assumptions, bearing on modifications of time and space relations and on the amount and kinds of information available within the group. That section presents concepts from five research groups that deal with the nature of communication and informa-tion processing in organizations, and how those activities might be influenced by technology.

The final section of the chapter considers three sets of contributions that attempt to provide an integration of theoretical ideas in this domain. One gives special emphasis to temporal issues in technologically enhanced work groups; a second gives special emphasis to the impact of technology on the organizations within which such groups are embedded. The third, drawing on our own prior work, employs a group theoretic perspective to integrate conceptions about time, tasks, and technology in work groups. Table 3.1 lists 17 research programs in the order in which their ideas are presented in this chapter.

GPSS: USING TECHNOLOGY TO SUPPORT GROUP MEETINGS

As noted earlier, efforts to improve group productivity have often taken the form of interventions by which persons managing the situation (group facilitators, researchers, group supervisors) could constrain and structure the communication within the group, the task information available to the group, and/or the form and sequence of task responses permitted and required of the group. Early intervention efforts of this kind are reflected in work identified under labels such as brainstorming (Diehl & Stroebe, 1987; Osborn, 1957), Delphi method (Dalkey, 1969), nominal group technique (NGT) (e.g., Van de Ven & Delbecq, 1974), multiattribute utility analysis (MAUA) (Eils & John, 1980), and many others. (For a summary, see McGrath, 1984.)

All of the systems used in those earlier decades, however, involved what might be called today manual technologies. They did not involve use of electronic or other high-tech devices. Computer-based group support systems are relatively recent developments, although they have proliferated in the last two decades. These more recent systems, based on electronic technology, have raised the sophistication of the hardware and software technology of group support systems by several orders of magnitude. One limitation of this area, however, is that many of those development efforts have not given much attention to issues concerning how

Table 3.1 Research Programs That Make Conceptual Contributions
Regarding Technology in Work Groups and Organizations

Conceptual formulations pertaining to:	*Research programs reviewed in this chapter:*
GPSS: Using technology to support group meetings (Assumption 1)	1 Nunamaker & colleagues (U. Arizona)
	2 Poole, DeSanctis, Dickson, & colleagues (U. Minnesota)
GCSS: Using technology to alter work and work relationships (Assumption 2)	3 Hiltz, Turoff, & colleagues (New Jersey Inst. Technology)
	4 Kiesler, Sproull, & colleagues (CMU)
	5 Bikson, Gutek, Eveland, & colleagues (Rand & Claremont)
	6 Kraut, Egido, Galegher, & colleagues (Bellcore & U. Arizona)
GISS & GXSS: Using technology for information acquisition and for external relations	7 Malone & colleagues (MIT)
	8 Ancona & colleagues (MIT)
	9 Gersick (UCLA)
Organizational context: The impact of technology on communication and information processes in organizations (Assumptions 2 & 3)	10 Williams & colleagues (University College, London)
	11 Daft & colleagues (Texas A&M)
	12 Fulk, Steinfield, Schmitz, & colleagues (USC)
	13 Rice & colleagues (USC & Rutgers)
	14 King, Star, & colleagues (UC Irvine)
Integrations: Time, tasks, and technology in work groups and organizations	15 Hesse & colleagues (U. Utah)
	16 Huber & colleagues (U. Texas)
	17 McGrath, Hollingshead, & colleagues (U. Illinois)

groups function, and how the technology may change the very nature of those groups. In this section, we review some of the conceptual formulations emanating from the two research groups that have led the development of highly sophisticated group performance support systems, while still giving attention to matters of group structure and process.

A General Framework for Studying Electronically Mediated Systems: Contributions of Nunamaker and Colleagues (University of Arizona)

One longtime and major contributor to research in this area of study has been the group working out of the Management Information Systems (MIS) department of the University of Arizona. The group was built and headed by Jay Nunamaker, and includes a number of senior members (some now contributing from other universities and research organizations): Alan Dennis, Joey George, Len Jessup, Joe Valacich, Doug Vogel, and others. That group is most noted for its extensive work on the development and application of GroupSystems, as well as for substantial empirical work testing the usefulness of those systems. Some of that empirical work is discussed in other parts of this book.

The Arizona group has also made some important conceptual contributions to this area of study. Specifically, they have laid out a rather broad conceptual framework regarding electronic support systems and their effects on work in groups. We will summarize, here, the main features of that framework (Dennis et al., 1988; Nunamaker, Dennis, Valacich, Vogel, & George, 1991).

They propose that such systems be termed *electronic meeting systems* (EMS) (Dennis et al., 1988), which they define as "an information technology-based environment that supports group meetings, which may be distributed geographically and temporally" (p. 593). Such an environment may include distributed facilities, computer hardware and software, audio and video technology, procedures, methodologies, facilitators or facilitation, and various kinds of databases. The tasks in which groups engage in those meetings may include communication, problem solving, issue discussion, negotiation, conflict resolution, systems analysis and design, and collaborative activities such as preparing, editing, and sharing documents.

The Arizona group discusses such systems in terms of three broad and interrelated facets that they label, respectively: group process and outcomes; methods; and the environment. The first facet (group process and outcomes) is used to identify a very broad range of constructs that needs to be taken into account in developing, using, and studying EMS:

characteristics of the group itself;
characteristics of the task on which the group is working;
the organizational context in which system use takes place;
the process through which the group utilizes the system; and
the outcomes resulting from system use.

The second and third facets (method and environment, respectively) subsume a number of features of the particular EMS systems being considered. For the method facet, which refers to the tools provided by the software support of the system and to the rules and procedures built into those tools, they identify three key issues: (a) whether the EMS system requires a facilitator, permits a facilitator, or precludes a facilitator; (b) whether group processing is sequential or parallel; and (c) whether the tools support single or multiple group sessions. For the environment facet, which refers to the total system (hardware and associated software), they stress two features: (a) whether group members are proximal or dispersed with respect to space and (b) whether group members are using the system synchronously or asynchronously with respect to time.

Building on the work of Steiner (1972), these researchers propose four ways in which EMS can contribute to "process gains" (Nunamaker, Dennis, Valacich, Vogel, & George, 1991) and thereby aid group performance:

1. Process structure: An EMS can impose a process-related structure that directs the pattern, timing, or content of the discussion (e.g., by

encouraging the group to adopt an agenda or a structured choice process such as NGT).
2. Process support: An EMS can provide a new electronic communication channel.
3. Outcome structure: An EMS can provide a structured technique for task analysis (e.g., a computer model to aid decisions).
4. Outcome support: An EMS can provide supporting information and computation (e.g., databases and data analysis packages).

We add the cautious note that each of these four ways can result in process losses as well as—or instead of—process gains. An effective assessment of any given EMS requires a comprehensive analysis of both positive and negative effects.

These formulations provide a fairly systematic (but by no means exhaustive) taxonomy of classes of variables that play a part in the operation of groups, with or without EMS. They provide an extensive checklist of potentially important factors that no one working in this area should overlook. These ideas will play into our discussions of conceptual contributions from other sources later in this chapter, as well as the presentations of our conceptual formulation (at the end of this chapter and in Chapter 5), which contains a modified and elaborated taxonomy.

Adaptive Structuration Theory: Contributions of Poole, DeSanctis, and Colleagues (University of Minnesota)

Some of the most powerful theory and research regarding group support systems has been generated by a group of researchers in several departments of the University of Minnesota, working with the SAMM group decision support system. The group has three key senior researchers (Gerardine DeSanctis, Gary Dickson, and M. Scott Poole) and a number of additional researchers, some of whom have carried their efforts to other universities and research organizations: Brent Gallupe, Michael Holmes, Fred Neiderman, Jonelle Roth, V. Sambamurthy, Dale Shannon, Rick Watson, Ilze Zigurs, and others.

This work represents the melding of two streams of research. On one hand, DeSanctis, Dickson, and some of their colleagues have an extensive history of behavioral science research on electronic support systems, especially the SAMM system—a unix-based "decision room." On the other hand, Poole, Roth, and some of their colleagues have an extensive history of developing and applying a microlevel theory of group process: *adaptive structuration theory* (AST). Combining these two streams of effort has provided a very powerful base for development of advanced electronic support systems, for sound empirical assessment of those systems, and for development of complex and sophisticated conceptual formulations about groups operating in those systems. Poole's theoretical work on groups, without regard to EMS, is extensive; some of it is covered elsewhere in this book. The discussion here focuses on the conceptual work that brings together group theory and EMS theory (e.g., Poole, 1991; Poole & DeSanctis, 1989, 1990).

Poole, DeSanctis, and their colleagues apply AST to the study of the class of EMS that are group decision support systems. (In Chapter 2, we refer to these as GPSS; generally, they are referred to as GDSS). GDSS combine communication, computer, and decision technologies to support decision making and related collaborative activities of work groups, including idea creation, message exchange, project planning, document preparation, mutual product creation, joint planning, and joint decision making.

AST stresses the importance of group interaction processes, both in determining group outcomes and in mediating the effects of any given technology. Essentially, a social technology (such as an EMS) presents a structure of rules and operations to a group. But the group does not just passively receive the technology in preexisting form; rather, the group actively adapts the technology to its own ends, resulting in a restructuring of the technology as it is meshed with the group's own interaction system. Thus a technology in use ought to be thought of as a set of social practices that emerge and evolve over time.

From this point of view, the structure of a group is not to be thought of as a permanent, concrete set of relations, either among the members, or between members and their tasks; rather, the structure is a patterning of group activities that results from a continuing process by which groups use the rules and resources available to them to produce and reproduce the apparently stable systems that are observed. That continuing process is called *adaptive structuration.*

The rules and resources that groups use in the structuration process are sometimes created by them ad lib; but more often they are appropriated by the group from the social context in which it is embedded. Both technology and context affect group processes and outcomes because they affect this appropriation process.

Appropriation is the process by which a group selects and gives meaning to features (i.e., rules and resources) of a social technology. It is through such appropriation that a group can import and use a new technology. But appropriation is not a passive process: Each group gives meaning to, and thereby adapts for its use, the rules and resources on which it draws.

Thus social systems are to be thought of as observable patterns of relations among individuals and collectivities. Structures are the rules and resources used to produce and reproduce these social systems (that is, these patterns of relations). Both the systems and the structures deserve research attention.

Study of effects in such systems must take into account:

1. the nature of the technology and the structure (rules and resources) it supplies;
2. the context, the structures (rules and resources) supplied by that context, and the influences of contextual factors on the use and reproduction of structures;
3. the nature of the interactive structuring process itself, including how users appropriate and adapt structures both from the available technological system and from their own past experience.

This body of work, applying adaptive structuration theory to electronically enhanced groups, provides a detailed and process-oriented exploration of these issues. It fits within some of the broad categories of the conceptual schema presented by the Arizona group, and provides a detailed and microlevel treatment of those categories. In that sense the two programs are complementary. AST also meshes well with the temporally oriented formulations we have developed and applied in this area (discussed later in this chapter and in Chapter 5). Indeed, our formulations have borrowed extensively from the work of the Minnesota group.

GCSS: USING TECHNOLOGY TO ALTER WORK AND WORK RELATIONSHIPS

This section deals with work that is related to the second of the assumptions noted above: that technology can help groups overcome time and space constraints on meetings, and thereby expand the kinds of groups that can be created. This assumption has provided a crucial reason for developing and using technological systems such as computer conferences and e-mail distribution lists as communication media for groups. Yet relatively little research attention has been given to the effects of such systems: effects of spatial and temporal dispersion of members on collaborative work in groups; effects of restrictions in communication modalities that accompany use of such systems; long-term effects that the creation of such dispersed groups can have on the organizations within which they are embedded; and so forth. Conceptual contributions from four programs that have given direct and extensive attention to those issues are discussed here. These researchers focus their study not so much on the use of technology to structure and support task performance of extant groups, but rather on its use to extend and modify the communication networks within which people are or can be connected to one another—hence to modify the very definition and conception of *a group*.

Human Communication via Computer: Contributions of Hiltz, Turoff, and Colleagues (New Jersey Institute of Technology)

When Starr Roxanne Hiltz and Murray Turoff (NJIT) published their seminal book, *The Network Nation: Human Communication via Computer*, in 1978, it literally opened up an area of research inquiry. It was one of the first books to deal systematically with the topic of groups communicating via computers, and certainly one of the first to publish empirical data on the operation of such systems. From our extensive review of the literature on the impact of technology on group processes, it is evident that this book provided a conceptual touchstone for the later work of many of the researchers whose work is reviewed in this book. The central ideas in Hiltz and Turoff's early book are echoed in the conceptual schemes of a number of the researchers whose work is displayed in this chapter. For example, Kiesler's group at Carnegie Mellon University have subsequently tested many of the hypotheses offered by Hiltz and Turoff, and most often have found evidence supporting those earlier predictions. Similarly, some of the ideas proffered in *The Network Nation* are echoed in concepts of adaptive structuration theory developed by Poole and associates (see discussion earlier in this chapter).

Because this work has had very broad influence on the field, it could fit in many places in our presentation of conceptual schemes. We have placed it here because most of the technology that they talk about relates to synchronous and asynchronous computer conferences (GCSS in our terminology). Hiltz and Turoff identified a number of the potential advantages and disadvantages of computer conferencing (as compared with face-to-face conferencing) that have been documented in later work by a variety of researchers. The proposed advantages include removal of time and distance barriers to the formation of groups; easy expansion of work group sizes without decreasing actual participation of other members; and several other services and options not available during face-to-face meetings, such as anonymity of group members and increased access to information via electronic technology (use of GISS in our terminology). Hiltz and Turoff recognized (as many did not in the halcyon days of this research area) that those potential advantages were escorted by new and potentially troublesome issues. For example, the increased information handling capability raises questions for work groups and organizations with regard to who can control access to information, who can regulate its flow, and the like. It also raises the specter of massive information overload and problems of information interpretation (see discussion of Daft's ideas about information richness and equivocality, later in this chapter).

Hiltz and Turoff were among the first to describe differences between face-to-face and computer-mediated interaction in terms of social and psychological processes, and to discuss the importance of task-media contingencies. Groups communicating via computer have a narrower band of available communication modalities; nonverbal and paraverbal modalities are not available. In some situations, such narrow-band communication may allow information to be communicated with more precision and less noise, and may allow rational judgment processes to operate in the group with less intrusion of nonrational considerations. In other situations or for other purposes, however, the computer conference may need to be supplemented by other media in which nonverbal and paraverbal modalities are available. This idea foreshadows Daft's work on information richness and task-media contingency (discussed later in chapter).

The mechanisms for turn taking in communication are also different in the two media. In face-to-face meetings, only one person can speak at a time, or else the group's discussion will become chaotic; and face-to-face groups practice an elaborate set of norms that produce a coherent flow. During synchronous computer conferences, all participants can "talk" simultaneously. This can sometimes lead to a chaotic sequencing of messages, and to overload. Hiltz and Turoff speculated that a new system of conventions and procedural rules (i.e., norms) for participation in computer conferences would be needed to produce the same kind of smooth flow of communication that one sees in face-to-face groups. They predicted that such a system would emerge as users, individually and collectively, developed experience with this still-new medium.

Hiltz and Turoff also described the impact of computer mediation on the group discussion and decision-making process. They saw pressure on group members to conform to the views of the group (majority) as one of the most important dysfunctional aspects of face-to-face decision-making groups. They hypothesized that computer-mediated groups would have more equal participation among members, and that participants would be less influenced by high-status members, because status cues will be much less salient in those groups. On the same basis, they predicted that computer-mediated decision groups would show less risky shift than face-to-face groups, and would be more susceptible to informational influence than to pressures for social consensus. They also predicted that intelligence and problem-solving abilities of members would be more highly correlated with influence in computer groups than in face-to-face groups dealing with the same kinds of tasks. Finally, they hypothesized that all of these differences would increase as group size increased. Most of these hypotheses have received empirical support in subsequent research by those investigators or others.

The Social Psychology of Computer Use:
Contributions of Kiesler, Sproull, and
Colleagues (Carnegie Mellon University)

One of the strongest bodies of research in this area has been carried out at Carnegie Mellon University. Sara Kiesler and Lee Sproull have been the senior researchers of that group, and there is a large roster of additional contributors (Tom Finholt, Vitaly Dubrovsky, Tim McGuire, Jane Siegel, Suzanne Weisband, and others), some of whom have begun to make contributions from other universities and research sites. The Kiesler-Sproull work has focused on social psychological level effects of the use of computer-mediated communication. Their work has explored the effects of electronic technology on the distribution of participation among members, on types of contributions (e.g., task and social, emotional, and nonemotional), and on user responses to the availability of such systems (e.g., amount and pattern of use when use is discretionary, user satisfaction as a function of experience and circumstances).

Kiesler and colleagues see electronic communication systems as having great potential to enhance and expand collaborative work, but recognize that those gains come with some major negative consequences. Among the gains are adding new information, making groups of physically dispersed people possible, and making forms of asynchronous social interaction possible. At the same time, such electronic systems (as currently implemented) remove substantial social information and eliminate much feedback (such as nonverbal and paraverbal cues); these can have both positive and negative influences on interaction process, task outcomes, and responses of the users. (See Kiesler & Sproull, 1992; Sproull & Kiesler, 1991b.)

These authors argue that computer-mediated communication tends to depersonalize the communication/interaction process, with several concomitant effects. Individuals tend to lose "mental sight" of their interaction partners; that is, they lose the very particularized kind of mental image of their audience that people ordinarily would have in face-to-face communication (and to a lesser degree in other media such as telephone or video communications). At the same time, they lose access to a variety of cues that provide feedback to members regarding the impact of their behavior on interaction partners, and that communicate the status and individuality of the participants. Therefore, participants concentrate more on the messages and less on the persons involved in the communication.

At the same time, Kiesler and colleagues argue, the messages themselves appear to be ephemeral (even though they may actually be systematically recorded by the computer system in a way permitting system managers to reproduce them). Hence individuals feel less committed to what they say, less concerned about it, and less worried about how it will be received by their communication partners. As a consequence, individuals engaged in computer-mediated group interaction tend to:

1. feel more anonymous and detect less individuality in their communication partners;
2. participate more equally (because low-status members are less inhibited);
3. focus more on task and instrumental aspects and less on personal and social aspects of interaction (because the context is depersonalized);
4. communicate more negative and more uninhibited messages (because they are less concerned with social norms that tend to regulate and "civilize" communication in face-to-face groups); and
5. experience more difficulty in attaining group consensus (both because of elimination of much interpersonal feedback, and because of reduced concern with social norms).

The Kiesler-Sproull group (and others) have demonstrated all of these postulated effects (computer-mediated groups showing more equal participation, more negative and uninhibited comments, more task focus, and so forth) in a number of experimental studies. These rather robust findings lend considerable credence to their theoretical postulations. (There are, however, plausible alternative theoretical interpretations of such findings.)

Kiesler and Sproull argue that organizations have implemented electronic communication systems without much thought to such social psychological aspects of work in groups, and that there are essentially no cross-organizational norms to guide social behavior in them. Organizations need to take steps to modulate some of the potentially negative effects of electronic mediation while still capitalizing on the positive ones. Kiesler and Sproull argue that organizations need to deliberately develop and implement sets of social norms designed to put back the social information that electronic mediation removes. But they caution that, even with such modifications, electronic communication is not necessarily the medium of choice for all groups under all conditions. They propose that face-to-face groups may be more effective, and even necessary, for tasks requiring complex and subtle multiparty negotiations; they suggest that many groups may be most effective if they make use of an appropriate blend of face-to-face and computer-mediated communication.

The Importance of the Implementation Process:
Contributions of Bikson, Gutek, Eveland, and
Colleagues (Rand/Claremont-CGS)

A group of researchers associated with Rand Corporation and with Claremont Graduate School—Tora Bikson, Barbara Gutek, and J. D. Eveland being the senior researchers of that group—have also made important empirical and conceptual contributions to this area of study. They have carried out extensive field studies of computer technology in use, often in asynchronous forms (such as e-mail distribution lists and computer bulletin boards). They have adopted a *technology transfer* model, and have given special emphasis to the importance of the implementation stage of the process.

Specifically, they argue that much of the impact of a given new technology on a given organization arises not from the features of the technology itself, but from the organizational policies and practices that constitute the context within which that new technology is implemented. This argument, of course, is quite congruent with the adaptive structuration arguments made by the Minnesota group (discussed earlier), namely: that groups adapt systems as they acquire (i.e., appropriate) them; and that it is in the using of the system that its actual structure, meaning, and consequences are determined. The work of the Rand group is notable for demonstrating these effects in field settings and on a relatively macrolevel scale.

The Importance of Informal Communication in Collaborative Work: Contributions of Kraut and Colleagues (Bellcore)

A group of researchers located at Bell Communications Research (Bellcore) and at the University of Arizona (Robert Kraut, Jolene Galegher, Carmen Egido, and others) have carried out a number of studies of collaborative work on intellectually demanding tasks (e.g., scientific research, writing). They stress the importance of informal communications (i.e., short, unplanned, unstructured interactions) in developing effective collaborations. These are especially important in the early (initiation) stage of the collaboration, but they also play an important role in the later (planning, execution, and wind down) stages of collaborative projects. These researchers note that most point-to-point communication technology, especially those that permit communication among spatially and temporally dispersed persons, involve preplanned (or at least intentional), relatively structured interactions with preselected communication partners. But most scientific collaborations begin as a consequence of unplanned (and unintended), unstructured interactions with communication partners who were casually rather than systematically chosen. These researchers see the effective development and execution of collaborative efforts as requiring both (a) technologies that encourage more spontaneous interactions, such as e-mail to some degree, and video windows (see Chapter 2); and (b) situations that permit the use of mixes of face-to-face and electronically mediated communication among potential collaborators.

GISS AND GXSS: INFORMATIONAL, TEMPORAL, AND INTERACTIONAL PROCESSES IN GROUPS

In this section, we present conceptions we regard as particularly useful in understanding the effects of informational processes, temporal processes, and interactive processes on work in groups with or without electronic technology. None of the work included here really deals with the impact of electronic technology, but this work covers in especially enlightening ways two of the functions that technology can serve in work groups. First, we present Malone's work on coordination. It involves the GISS function; that is, it analyzes how a work group's interdependence (coordination) connects with its information-processing technology. Then we present two sets of conceptions that concern the GXSS function. One is the work of Ancona and colleagues, which deals with how work groups handle relations with their embedding organizational contexts. The other is the work of Gersick on the impact of the temporal context on how work groups carry out their tasks.

Coordination Theory: Contributions of
Malone and Colleagues (MIT)

Tom Malone and his colleagues at the Massachusetts Institute of Technology have provided a number of conceptual contributions regarding information processing in organizations. (See Malone, 1988; Malone & Crowston, 1990.) They have championed what they refer to as *coordination theory*. For Malone and colleagues, co-ordination entails whatever two or more actors must do, when they are doing a task together, that they would not have to do if doing the task alone. Actors, here, could be individuals, or computers, or groups. (In some senses, this is a definition of the coordination part of Steiner's [1972] process losses, which was discussed in Chapter 1 and will be discussed again later.)

Malone and colleagues analyze a number of different schemes for coordination. They draw attention to an inherent trade-off between flexibility and efficiency in all systems. On one hand, the desire for efficiency of operation drives increasing specialization of function and standardization of task performance procedures. On the other hand, the need for the system to deal effectively with unusual cases—nonstandard inputs, defective materials, abnormalities of timing and placing—drives a need to incorporate flexibility of procedures into the system. Those two are directly conflicting desiderata.

Malone and colleagues analyze a number of aspects of coordination at many levels. These include:

1. alternative ways of segmenting the total set of tasks/projects in which the organization is engaged (e.g., organizing work by product vs. by function vs. in a product-by-function matrix organization);
2. different functions that coordination activities can serve for the organization (e.g., allocation of scarce resources, communication of intermediate results, etc.);
3. different patterns of connection among individuals and units by which coordination can be carried out (e.g., mutual adjustment, direct supervision, standardization, etc.);
4. different systems for coordination (e.g., hierarchies, augmented hierarchies, markets, etc.); and
5. multiple criteria for evaluating coordination (e.g., flexibility, efficiency).

Malone's work provides some basic theoretical underpinnings for the interaction between technology and information processing. But even though the term *coordination* implies multiple actors, Malone's work does not deal specifically with groups in action, and does not give much emphasis to temporal issues.

Internal and External Relations of Work Groups:
Contributions of Ancona and Colleagues (MIT)

Deborah Ancona and her colleagues at MIT argue, on the basis of extensive empirical research, that how groups manage their external relations (i.e., communications with persons and units who are outside the group, in the embedding organization and/or its operating environment) is as important to group success as how they deal with internal processes. Groups cannot remain isolated from the organizational and environmental context within which they exist, because they depend on that context for resources. Thus, in addition to the need for coordination within the group, each work group also continually needs to deal with its relations to the embedding organization and operating environment. (This idea is commensurate with Poole's conceptions of the appropriation process; see prior discussion.) Those external relations involve process links of various kinds: negotiation, information exchange, scanning, profile management, buffering, and so forth.

The relative importance of effective management of internal processes versus effective management of external relations varies as a function of the performance coordination demands of the group's tasks and the level and variability of demands in its environment. Furthermore, the group composition and group process requirements of the two functions often are dramatically different, even contradictory. A high level of effective internal coordination is often produced by homogeneity of members, attitude conformity, and standardization of action. Effective relations with the environment often requires heterogeneity of membership and of attitudes, and high levels of receptivity to environmental scanning, modeling, and (two-way) influence. (Part of this is related to Malone's conception of an inherent trade-off between efficiency and flexibility.)

Management of external relations involves three general strategies:

1. initiating transactions with people outside the group to import or export information, resources, or support;
2. responding to such initiations by people outside the group; and
3. defining who is and is not in the group.

There are different patterns of activities, which can be characterized as roles, associated with each of these strategies:

- Strategy 1 characterizes the activities of two roles:

  Scout, which involves modeling, information and resource gathering, detecting, and feedback seeking; and

  Ambassador, which involves opening communication channels, in-
  forming others of group progress, coordinating and negotiating,
  and influencing the external world with regard to the group.

- Strategy 2 characterizes the activities of two other roles:

  Sentry, which involves monitoring and determining from whom
  to accept input, how much of it to accept, the form that input must
  be in, and when the flow must stop; and

  Guard, which involves monitoring information and resources that
  are requested from the group, and determining how the group will
  respond to those requests.

- Strategy 3 characterizes the impact of individuals who can be labeled
  as immigrants, captives, and emigrants. The presence or absence of
  these individuals in the group changes the actual membership of the
  group:

  Immigrant refers to an outsider who has been induced to voluntar-
  ily join the group;

  Captive refers to a person assigned to the group; and

  Emigrant refers to a group member who leaves the group.

This work is important in part because it is one of the few bodies
of work that recognizes the importance of external relations. Those
processes also involve communication links, and could involve
technology. However, although Ancona and colleagues deal with
group processes, they do not deal in any specific way with technology or with temporal issues.

Punctuated Equilibrium in Work Groups:
Contributions of Gersick (UCLA)

Connie Gersick at the University of California, Los Angeles has
made an important conceptual contribution regarding the temporal course of group task performance. She deals with groups that
are designed to carry out a single project of substantial size, and to

do so by a predetermined deadline: a *task force* (McGrath, 1984). Based on both field and laboratory research (Gersick, 1988, 1989), she postulates that such groups carry out projects with a temporal pattern characterized by five temporally ordered segments: three brief but crucial transition periods separated by two relatively long but less turbulent work periods. She labels this pattern a *punctuated equilibrium*. The boundaries of these five phases are defined, not by work completed, but by the amount of time that has passed (or by the two jointly). The initial start-up phase is characterized by a more or less "thoughtless" adoption of goals and of a strategy for work. This is followed by a period of work using that strategy, lasting until almost exactly the midpoint of the group's predetermined life span. The midpoint transition involves a complete reexamination (and often, a drastic modification) of the group's work, strategy, and goals. This is followed by another period of work, using the newly adopted strategy and goals, and then by a relatively brief ending transition during which the group wraps up both its project and its existence.

The uniformity with which all of Gersick's groups, in both of two studies (one field, one lab), exhibited the midpoint transition at exactly the middle of their life spans—even though those life spans varied from 2 hours to 4 months—suggests that her conception of the flow of work in groups offers a model for a very robust set of temporal patterning phenomena. These studies do not deal with technology, nor are they concerned with information processing in any detail; but they make a potentially crucial contribution regarding temporal processes in groups.

ORGANIZATIONAL CONTEXT: THE IMPACT OF TECHNOLOGY ON COMMUNICATION AND INFORMATION PROCESSES IN ORGANIZATIONS

The work discussed in this section reflects both the second assumption (about modifying time and space relations) and the third assumption (about modifying the amount and kinds of information available within the group). It presents concepts from five research groups that deal with how the potential amount and content of communication differs for various communication media. Some of these conceptual contributions center around the idea that technology brings two opposite sets of consequences. On one hand, technology extends the range of possible communicators beyond the time and space barriers imposed on face-to-face groups (see prior discussion). At the same time, it restricts the modalities through which those individuals can communicate with one another. Different theorists have given different names to this issue and to the dimensions on which communication media differ, but all have been in agreement that this restriction of modalities can have both favorable and adverse effects on the work of groups.

The conceptual contributions presented in this section do not deal directly with work groups, nor with the effects of technology on such groups; and they do not deal very extensively with temporal issues. Nevertheless, these formulations are at least indirectly relevant to the topic at hand, because they provide some conceptual underpinnings to aid our understanding of organizational level issues pertinent to communication and information processing in work groups.

Social Presence and Technological Impact: Contributions by Williams and Colleagues (University College, London)

Some of the earliest work in this research domain was carried out by Ederyn Williams and his colleagues. Portions were done before computer use was widespread; hence that earlier work dealt with technological systems other than computers, such as telephone, video, and teletype.

These researchers (Short, Williams, & Christie, 1976) draw on an even earlier telecommunications impact model (Reid, 1971), but build beyond it to present a social presence model that seems to be a precursor of (a) Daft's work on media richness (discussed later), (b) some of the concepts in the work of the Kiesler group (described previously), and (c) some of the concepts in our own formulations (discussed later in this chapter and in Chapter 5).

Williams and colleagues propose a social presence model to predict the media that individuals will use for certain types of interaction. Social presence refers to the degree of salience of the other person in the interaction, hence the salience of the interpersonal relationship involved in the interaction. They regard social presence as a quality inherent in the medium. They hypothesize that media differ in this quality, and that individuals are aware of this quality of media and use it as part of the basis for their choice of media for particular types of interaction. Specifically, they predict that individuals will avoid a given medium for a given type of interaction if they perceive that medium as not providing a high enough degree of social presence for that type of interaction. They also predict that communications via media low in social presence will be more task oriented (that is, have more task content relative to interpersonal content) than face-to-face communication. (Although Williams and associates regard social presence as a quality inherent in the medium, they measure it in terms of individual perceptions, usually using semantic differential scales, and hence convert it from an objective to a subjective property of the communication system.)

Equivocality, Uncertainty, and Information Richness:
Contributions of Daft and Colleagues (Texas A&M)

Among the many important conceptual contributions of Richard Daft and colleagues at Texas A&M University, the ones most pertinent here have to do with information processing and communication media in organizations. Daft and his colleagues (Daft & Lengel, 1986) have proposed the idea that information can be equivocal, in addition to or instead of being uncertain or ambiguous. They have used that idea to analyze the differential "information richness" of various tasks and media within organizational settings, and to postulate the importance of a good match between media and tasks on that dimension.

In their usage, a situation is uncertain or ambiguous when a given group or person has only limited information available about that situation at a given time, but that missing information could, in principle, be obtained. A situation is equivocal, on the other hand, when it can be viewed from more than one perspective and can be taken to have more than one meaning. In such a situation, no amount of searching can lead to additional information that will delimit the situation to a single meaning, because such definitive information does not and in principle cannot exist.

Daft and Lengel argue that structure can be designed to reduce equivocality, or to provide data to reduce uncertainty, or to do both (or neither), depending on organizational needs. Daft and Lengel further propose that different forms of communication (e.g., written memos, group meetings) differ in the "richness" of the information that they provide, and thereby in their capacity to reduce equivocality (rather than just to reduce uncertainty). They propose seven structural mechanisms (i.e., communication methods), ordered along a continuum in terms of their capacity for resolving equivocality versus for reducing uncertainty (hence along an information richness continuum): group meetings, integrators, direct (person-to-person) contact, planning, special reports, formal information systems, and rules and regulations. Daft and Lengel argue that managers need to (and do) use different communication methods (of appropriate degrees of richness) to deal with situations that differ in equivocality/uncertainty. Hence different types of technology, which differ in the richness of the information they communicate, need to be used for different types of organizational decisions.

Information richness is a key concept in their schema. The more equivocality a situation involves, the richer the information required to deal with it. Richness seems to subsume much of what Williams and colleagues (see prior discussion), Kiesler and colleagues (see prior discussion), McGrath and Hollingshead (see later discussion), and others have talked about as social cues, social presence, redundancy, feedback, and the like. However, Kiesler and others propose that lack of such richness (i.e., low social presence) is part of a set of conditions that leads to depersonalization and a number of associated effects: more equal participation, more negative and uninhibited communication, more difficulty in reaching consensus, and so on. Such complex effects of lack of richness of information do not seem to be in accord with the effects that Daft and Lengel assign to the uncertainty reduction end of their continuum. These issues deserve further exploration. Daft and Lengel's work provides some basic theoretical underpinnings regarding the interface between technology and information processing, but does not deal with either groups or temporal issues.

Social Influence Theory: Contributions of Fulk, Steinfield, Schmitz, and Colleagues (USC)

Janet Fulk, Joseph Schmitz, and Charles Steinfield (e.g., Fulk, Schmitz, & Steinfield, 1990; Schmitz & Fulk, 1991) focus on media selection, building on the work of Daft and colleagues (and the prior work of Williams and colleagues). They cast that work within a social influence model, insisting that social interaction in the workplace shapes the creation of shared meanings, and that those shared meanings provide an important basis for shared patterns of media selection. (Those ideas are quite in accord with Poole's work on adaptive structuration and the appropriation process.)

These researchers argue that the Daft model is more normative than descriptive of communication patterns in organizations. They argue for the importance of measurement of individual perceptions of the information richness of various media, rather than relying solely on an assessment of its objective richness (see prior discussion of Williams's work). Such objective features of media richness do influence individual perceptions of media richness, but there are other sources of such influence (e.g., a set of "media expertise" factors such as computer experience and keyboard facility).

The social influence model proposes that media perceptions and use (a) are subject to social influence; (b) may be subjectively or retrospectively rationalized; (c) are not necessarily aimed at maximizing efficiency (echoing Malone's efficiency/flexibility trade-off); and (d) may be designed to preserve or create ambiguity to achieve strategic goals (in accord with Daft's conceptions). This work, as does Williams's and Daft's, deals with information processing and communication media (hence technology), but not with groups or with temporal issues.

Communication in Organizations as Complex Patterns of Interaction: Contributions of Rice and Colleagues (USC and Rutgers)

Ron Rice, initially working out of USC and more recently at Rutgers (e.g., Rice, 1989, 1990; Rice & Shook, 1990a), emphasizes that there has been a major shift in the conceptualization of the communication process, partly brought about by trying to understand communication in groups interacting with technology. That shift has been from a "straight line" concept of communication as "a source sending a message to a target," to a more complex network conception of communication as a complex process of interaction and convergence. There has been a concomitant shift in the unit of analysis from the message to the communication relationship and the pattern of interaction.

Rice argues that computer-mediated communication systems (CMC) have the potential to alter some of the structures, constraints, and connectivity possibilities associated with face-to-face communication, and thereby foster more efficient communication and new kinds of interaction. Specifically, CMC can be used to structure communication processes, can alter some of the spatial, temporal, and social constraints that operate in the communication process, and can connect users in diverse locations.

This work notes, but does not give much emphasis to, the idea that all of these changes in structure, constraints, and connectivity carry both benefits and costs for the collaborative work of groups. This work deals with communication and technology, but does not really treat group process or temporal issues. (Please note that Rice and his colleagues have made some major empirical and integrative contributions with respect to voice-messaging systems and other technologies besides computer-mediated communication.)

Noshir Contractor (trained at USC, now at University of Illinois) has done work that extends Rice's approach to temporal and interactional issues, and also ties it to the GDSS area discussed in the first section of this chapter. He has applied network analysis methods and self-organizing systems theory (SOST) to study how groups appropriate group decision support systems, and the dynamic effects of these systems on groups (Contractor & Siebold, 1993). This work examines temporal issues (the effects of technology change and of increasing experience with a technology) at the level of the work group as a quasi-independently functioning system.

Communication Within Organizations:
Contributions of King, Star, and Colleagues (UC Irvine)

Among a number of contributions by John King, S. Leigh Star, and colleagues at the University of California at Irvine, King and Star (1990) attempt to extend the use of decision support systems (DSS) from individual and group level decisions to organizational level decisions (ODSS). King and Star argue that features of DSS that are important at group levels may not apply or may even be dysfunctional at organizational levels. ODSS differ from GDSS in at least four important respects:

1. Organizations often address issues of larger social consequences and gravity.
2. Organizational decision making is usually representative rather than inclusive of opinions of all members (i.e., not everyone gets a direct "say").
3. Organizational processes are usually less socially grounded than group processes (i.e., decision makers putatively approach them with more objectivity, less emotion, and less concern for social aspects).
4. Organizational decision processes are usually more formal than group decision processes.

Even with these differences, King and Star argue that ODSS ought to be constructed to preserve two important features of current GDSS: (a) a mechanism for maintenance of articulated due process (i.e., all parties explicitly get an input, the decision rule is explicit, and so forth); and (b) the establishment of boundary objects. Even though their treatment of boundary objects is at an organizational level (see following), it is in their elaboration of the boundary objects concept that King and Star's work is most relevant in the present context.

One of the major ways in which groups (and individuals) with heterogeneous interests collaborate is through the joint creation of boundary objects: bundles of information that have the same boundaries (i.e., the same information items are included) for all of a set of multiple collaborating groups, even though those bundles have contents and uses that are quite different when viewed from the different perspectives of each of those groups. King and Star distinguish four types of boundary objects:

1. *Repositories* are ordered "piles" of objects indexed in a standardized way (e.g., libraries and data archives), so they can be useful to people who partition problems using different units of analysis.
2. *Ideal types* are diagrams, atlases, or other descriptions that are not necessarily accurate in complete detail but are a means for communicating symbolically (e.g., blueprints).
3. *Coincident boundaries* are common objects that have the same boundaries but different internal contents from the perspective of different users (e.g., detailed production records for a given plant in a given year would contain different contents for the purposes of marketing, purchasing, and production departments).
4. *Standardized forms* are methods for communication in a common language across diverse (and dispersed) work groups.

The importance of such common boundary objects increases, and the relative usefulness of different kinds of boundary objects is likely to change, as the size and diversity of organizational components increases.

INTEGRATIONS: THE INTERPLAY
OF TIME, TASKS, AND TECHNOLOGY
IN WORK GROUPS AND ORGANIZATIONS

In this final section we present three sets of contributions, each of which represents an attempt at integration of a wide range of ideas in this domain but from three different perspectives. First, we present an outline of Hesse and colleagues' integration from the perspective of a transactional theory. Second, we present a brief sketch of Huber's theory of the impact of technology on development, intelligence, and decisions of organizations. Third, we present ideas drawn from our own past work, which offer a group theoretic perspective on how technology affects informational, interactional, and temporal processes in work groups.

A Transactional View of Computer Mediation:
Contributions of Hesse and Colleagues (University of Utah)

Brad Hesse, Carol Werner, and Irwin Altman at the University of Utah have presented a transactional analysis of temporal aspects of communication in computer-mediated groups that stands as one of the few treatments in this domain that gives substantial attention to temporal factors, to group process issues, and to the impact of technology. (Hesse has made further contributions in this domain, at Carnegie Mellon University and at The American Institutes for Research.)

In the transactional view, events (including communication patterns) are best regarded holistically, and are characterized by certain inherent temporal properties. Computer-mediated communication systems provide a distinctive temporal context; hence events in that context are likely to differ on some or all of those temporal properties.

Hesse, Werner, and Altman (1990) propose that time operates in both linear and cyclical patterns in all human interactions. Within each of these, events are characterized by four main temporal properties: temporal scale, sequencing, pace, and salience.

Temporal scale refers to the order of magnitude of the crucial temporal features of the behavior patterns of concern, ranging from seconds to very long-term patterns. Synchronous computer communication puts stringent limits on the amount of information that can be transmitted in a given transaction (because typing is slower than speaking). In contrast, asynchronous systems increase flexibility with respect to time scale. Regarding sequence: Computer mediation disrupts sequencing in communication, and that may lead to decreases in predictability, decreases in satisfaction, and increases in interpersonal friction. Regarding pace: Computer mediation affects pace (rate) differently for different aspects of the communication process. It makes generation of messages slower (typing is slower than speaking), but makes transmission faster and makes reception of a given message faster (i.e., reading is faster than listening).

Salience refers to whether the social unit and action pattern are oriented toward future, present, or past. Hesse, Werner, and Altman (1990) speculate that because the social presence of the other, hence the continuing relationship, past and future, is less salient, computer-mediated communication may be more present oriented (by default).

These temporal issues (and a number of others that we will add later) are important aspects of communication, and play a role in differentiating computer-mediated from face-to-face interaction in groups. They need to be taken into account in research in this domain.

Impact of Information Technologies on Organizations:
Contributions of Huber and Colleagues (University of Texas)

George Huber, at the University of Texas, has presented what is perhaps the broadest and most comprehensive theoretical formulation in this area. It focuses on the organizational level, although it gives some attention to group structure and process as well. It is concerned with the long-run impact of new and advanced technologies (Huber, 1990), including electronic technologies (Huber, Valacich, & Jessup, 1993), on the development of the organization itself, on its information processing and intelligence, and on its decisions.

Huber offers 14 propositions, structured in terms of five key constructs, from which he generates the following overall themes: Availability of advanced technology fosters its use, which in turn provides increased information accessibility (from both inside and outside the organization or work group). That, in turn, produces changes in organizational structure. The increased information accessibility and the consequent changes in organizational structure together lead to improvements in the effectiveness of intelligence development and decision making.

Huber's is a normative theory, in a sense; perhaps it is more accurate to say that his theory seems to presume a "frictionless system." He explicitly assumes that organizations are composed of rational actors. He does not deny the existence of political (or other nonrational) processes, but assumes that individuals will use technology to advance both their own and the organization's interests; that is, that they will act rationally, and therefore that available technology will be put to use (and have positive effects on the organization and its decisions). He cites empirical (and sometimes anecdotal) support for the various propositions and concepts that he proposes, putting less emphasis on the possibility of negative effects ensuing from the same "driving forces." Overall, it is impressive in its scope and directness, and warrants extensive and systematic empirical tests of its propositions.

Time, Tasks, and Technology in Work Groups:
Contributions of McGrath, Hollingshead, and
Colleagues (University of Illinois)

In this section we present our conceptual contributions to this domain. Mainly, those contributions have involved two themes: (a) an effort to develop and apply a dynamic theory of work groups in which technology and time play key roles along with task, group, and membership factors; and (b) an insistence that research in this area should use an approach that is as comprehensive as possible, conceptually, methodologically, and substantively. Contributors to this body of work include Holly Arrow, Gail Futoran, Deborah Gruenfeld, David Harrison, Janice Kelly, Kathleen O'Connor, and Susan Straus, as well as Andrea Hollingshead and Joseph McGrath, the authors of this book.

Underlying the presentation here is a general schema or theory about groups, called *time, interaction, and performance* (TIP) theory. TIP theory is presented in detail elsewhere (see McGrath, 1990, 1991; McGrath & Gruenfeld, 1993); it will be outlined briefly below, to provide a point of entry for our discussions of a number of theoretical issues.

The Nature of Groups

TIP theory regards groups as continuously and simultaneously engaged in three major functions: production, member support, and group well-being. These functions represent, respectively, contributions of the group to its embedding organization, contributions of the group to its participating members, and contributions of the group to its own continued functioning as an intact social unit.

Groups carry out those functions by means of activities in one or another of four modes. The general forms as shown in Figure 3.1 are:

Mode I: Inception of a project (goal choice);
Mode II: Solution of technical issues (means choice);
Mode III: Resolution of conflict (i.e., of political rather than technical issues); and
Mode IV: Execution of the performance requirements of the project.

Modes transcend functions, and there are parallel but distinguishable forms of the modes within each of the three functions. Furthermore, the modes are not a fixed sequence of phases, but rather four potential forms of activity by which each of the functions can be pursued in relation to any given project. Groups carry out their projects by means of time/activity paths that consist of mode/function sequences. Every (completed) project involves at least Modes I and IV for the production function (i.e., the group gets a project and executes it). Any given case may or may not involve Modes II and III for the production function (i.e., attempts to solve technical issues or resolve political issues). It also may or may not involve some or all modes of activity with respect to the member support and group well-being functions (e.g., a redistribution of task roles, a reallocation of status or payoff relations, and recruitment and socialization of a new member).

| | FUNCTIONS | | |
MODES	Production	Member Support	Well-being
Mode I Inception	Project Selection/ Assignment	Member Participation Choice	Group Interaction Choice
Mode II Problem Solving	Technical Problem Solving	Position/ Status Attainments	Role Network Definition
Mode III Conflict Resolution	Policy Conflict Resolution	Contribution/ Payoff Relationships	Power/ Payoff Distribution
Mode IV Execution	Performance	Participation	Interaction

Figure 3.1. Modes and Functions
SOURCE: McGrath (1991). Copyright © 1991 Sage Publications, Inc.

Temporal Aspects of Groups

TIP theory deals with temporal aspects of group interaction and performance at several levels. It concerns the flow of work at the relative macrolevels that are sometimes discussed in terms of phases of performance or stages of group development (overlapping with work of Poole and colleagues, and of Gersick, discussed earlier in this chapter). These have to do with the group's ability to match time units and activity requirements of its projects in a smooth and coordinated pattern. The model also deals with temporal factors at a more microlevel, having to do with coordination or synchronization of activities (overlapping with Malone's work on coordination). There is an emphasis in TIP theory on processes that bring about entrainment and mutual entrainment (that is, coordination and synchronization) of temporal patterns of behavior within groups.

TIP theory also deals with temporal factors at a still more micro-level, involving the flow of information, uncertainty, redundancy, and the like, on one hand, and the dynamics of interpersonal interaction among group members on the other (overlapping with issues raised by Daft and colleagues, and by Kiesler and colleagues). At this level, the model considers each activity of a group member in terms of its contribution to the group's production, well-being, and member support functions. It specifies how particular observable behaviors relate to smooth or disrupted interaction processes, high or low rates of productivity, and high or low quality of task performance.

Complexity of Group Processes

In TIP theory, natural groups are involved in a complex set of activities. At any given time, any given natural group is likely to be engaged in more than one project, and to be pursuing each of those projects by means of some sequences of modes of activity with respect to each of the three functions. Study of natural groups thus requires a complex set of observational and conceptual tools.

The performance of a given group in an organization is contingent on a number of sets of factors having to do with (a) attributes of the group's members; (b) the group's composition, structure, and patterns of interaction, as well as its developmental history; (c) the group's assigned or selected tasks/projects/objectives, and the tools and procedures by which it will carry out those tasks; and (d) the group's organizational, physical, and temporal environment.

TIP Theory and Technology

TIP theory is a general theory of groups, rather than one developed for study of technology in groups. The propositions of TIP theory together provide a solid foundation for a fairly comprehensive conception of the flow of interaction and information in work groups in general. Nevertheless, that theory does have certain important implications for technology and its uses. Indeed, in one of its presentations (see McGrath, 1990) TIP theory contained a set of propositions that were tentative hypotheses about the impact of technology on the flow of work in groups. These propositions included:

1. Specification of 10 hypothetical or implicit rules by which ordinary face-to-face interaction seems to be structured, and discussion of a variety of ways in which the structure of communication under various forms of technologically mediated interaction is likely to violate or ignore those rules.
2. Identification of seven categories of technology that potentially could be used in work groups. The categories were ordered along a dual continuum that simultaneously reflects, on one hand, the time-and-space bridging expansions of communication connections, and on the other hand, the constriction of modalities by which communication can take place. This dual continuum has conflicting influences on the flow of work in groups.
3. Specification of several major classes of effects on informational, temporal, and interactional processes, some positive and some negative in direction, that are likely to result from technology in groups.

These initial classifications and tentative hypotheses proved to be useful but too simplistic. Our extensive review of the literature showed that a number of researchers have presented concepts and perspectives (see earlier parts of this chapter) that allowed us to take our own conceptual formulations considerably beyond our starting point (as presented in McGrath, 1990, and outlined above). Some of those extensions and complexities are discussed next.

Technology and Tasks

Group interaction and performance is greatly affected by the type and difficulty of the tasks that the group is performing. Furthermore, effects of technology on group interaction and performance interact with task type. Hence appreciating the effects of various kinds of technology on collaborative work in groups requires reckoning with effects of variations in task.

A task classification schema drawn from earlier work (McGrath, 1984) provides a good starting place for that consideration. That schema (see Figure 3.2) proposes that all group tasks can be categorized as one or another of four main types (each with two subtypes). The four main task types, related to each other as the four

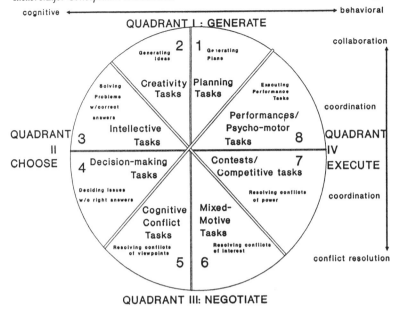

Figure 3.2. Group Task Circumplex
SOURCE: Joseph E. McGrath, *Groups, Interaction and Performance,* © 1984, p. 61. Adapted by permission of Prentice Hall, Englewood Cliffs, NJ.

quadrants of a circumplex structure, are identified by the main performance process that each entails: I, to generate (ideas or plans); II, to choose (a correct answer or a preferred solution); III, to negotiate (conflicting views or conflicting interests); and IV, to execute (in competition with an opponent or in competition against external performance standards).

From an information processing point of view, these task types differ in terms of the degree to which effective performance on them depends only on the transmission of information among members of the group, or also requires the transmission of values, interests, personal commitments, and the like. They differ, that is, in the degree of "media richness" (Daft & Lengel, 1986) required for their accomplishment. It is likely that the effects of any given form of computer mediation will depend on the type of task that the group is doing (as well as on various characteristics of the group itself).

Structuring Information and Action in Work Groups

Many forms of technology for collaborative work in groups involve what we termed, in Chapter 2, GCSS; that is, they mediate intragroup communication and, to some degree, place limits on, and structure, the communication process itself. They necessarily limit channels and modalities by which members can communicate with one another, and to some degree limit the syntactical forms by which members can communicate via those available channels. Even the "unmediated" interaction of face-to-face groups imposes some limitations and structuring on group communication processes and other aspects of group work, often by implicit though powerful social norms. (The 10 implicit rules of face-to-face communication presented in McGrath, 1990, noted earlier, reflect such norms for the communication process.)

Many technologies for work groups provide both a GCSS and a GPSS; that is, they structure task performance as well as intragroup communication. There are a variety of other ways in which some technologies limit and structure the group's performance: by removing one or more of the performance processes from the group's performance responsibility; by structuring the amount and form of information available to the group; and/or by structuring the form and sequence of responses by which the group can do its work.

Decision support systems are a case in point. They often embed tools for structuring the generation of ideas, for setting an agenda, for attaining consensus, and so on, in addition to providing a system by which group members may communicate with one another. Furthermore, such systems sometimes impose highly constrained response formats on the group (e.g., requiring them to pick a single answer from a set of preestablished alternatives, rather than allowing the group to generate and modify its own alternatives, and then to choose the form and pattern of response by which to convey that choice). Any systematic analysis of the impact of computer mediation in groups must take into account the impact of such prior structuring of task activity, as well as modifications of communication, which arise from use of any given computer mediation system.

The four quadrants of the task circumplex mentioned previously can help organize the forms in which task performance of work groups can be constrained by prior structuring (by either computer-based media or manual means). Most of the forms of task structuring used in computer-mediated groups have to do with the processes underlying one or another of those four quadrants:

Quadrant I: Some forms of task structuring involve procedures that structure how the group goes about its generating activities, for example: brainstorming; goal-setting procedures; agenda setting; procedures for acquiring or generating alternatives, ideas, goals, plans; and so on.

Quadrant II: Other forms of task structuring involve procedures that structure how the group goes about its choosing activities, for example: Delphi; NGT; procedures for aggregating and weighting preference, for facilitating "rational" choices among "right answers," for selecting and using algorithms to determine satisficing or optimizing solutions, and for choosing among alternatives.

Quadrant III: Other forms of task structuring involve procedures that structure how the group goes about its negotiating activities, such as multiattribute utility analysis; negotiation-structuring protocols; procedures for resolving conflicting interests; and voting procedures to force resolution of conflicting views.

Quadrant IV: Still other forms of task structuring involve procedures that structure how the group carries out its executing activities, for example: procedures that require the group to generate its product in a specified response form, such as a rank order or a probability estimate, or that limit modalities of response to be used in generating the product, or that constrain response sequences, or that set criteria for timing, quality, and form of the product.

Because TIP theory highlights the rather complex processes by which groups form, organize, acquire tasks/purposes, and carry out those tasks, then in principle it should help specify which processes are and which are not affected by any given technological system. Furthermore, because different kinds of technological systems have impact on different parts of group process, according to TIP theory, they should have different patterns of effects (both positive and negative) depending on what task(s) the group is doing. Hence TIP theory emphasizes the likelihood that system performance will be a joint function of a number of features (of group, task, situation) in interaction with a given form of technology.

Those effects on system performance are reflected in group process as well as in task products, and thus TIP theory provides a basis for interpretation of some of the findings about group process in computer-mediated versus face-to-face groups. For example: TIP theory suggests that the high level of task focus often found in computer-mediated groups (compared with face-to-face groups) reflects an overconcentration on the productivity function, often on the "default path" (Mode I followed by Mode IV), to the exclusion of other production function modes (II or III), and to the exclusion of attention to the group well-being and member support functions. Under some circumstances, doing so could improve short-term task performance without undue harm to longer run considerations. For example: Groups with no expectations about future interaction, as would be the case with many of the groups studied in experimental contexts, might benefit from a total focus on the task. Such groups would have far less need to attend to group well-being and member support functions than continuing groups do.

But under other circumstances, such overconcentration on execution of the production task could not only harm longer-term group well-being and member support considerations, but also could be detrimental to concurrent task performance effectiveness itself (e.g., when technical problem-solving issues and/or conflict resolution issues are overlooked by the group in its zeal to focus solely on task and product). Moreover, findings regarding a difference in distribution of participation among group members, with computer groups showing more equal rates of participation, can be viewed, in TIP theory, either as an efficient use of group resources, or as an inefficient form of task performance (lack of an efficient division of labor), depending on the distribution of information and task expertise among members.

Changes Over Time

TIP theory insists on treating groups as complex dynamic systems, rather than taking a more static focus. Some of the issues discussed earlier take on a different perspective when viewed from such a dynamic standpoint. TIP theory posits that natural groups are involved in a rather complex set of activities. At any given time, any given natural group is likely to be engaged in more than one project, and to be pursuing each of those projects by means of some sequence of modes of activity with respect to each of three functions. Thus study of the work of such natural groups requires a complex set of observational tools and a complex set of expectations about the meanings of the behaviors that are likely to be observed.

In contrast to this complexity, much research on technology in groups (and much research on group behavior in general) seems to be based on an overly simplistic set of expectations about likely behaviors and their meanings. Research on technology and groups to date has focused almost exclusively on the production function of those groups. Relatively little attention has been paid to how, and how well, those groups socialize, train, and support their members, nor to how, and how well, those groups take care of their own system maintenance.

Moreover, much of the research on technology and groups has been done under the apparent assumption that those groups were engaged in only one task or project: the one assigned by or attended to by the researchers. In such research, all activity that does not directly contribute to the performance of that task usually is regarded as evidence of inefficiency of that group.

Furthermore, much of that research also has been done on the apparent assumption that those work groups were—or ought to be—carrying out that single (assigned) task or project by means of some idealized sequence of problem-solving phases (i.e., a fixed sequence of modes of activity of the production function). In such research, activity that departs from that idealized sequence of phases is likely to be regarded as evidence of inefficiency or inadequacy of that work group (i.e., as the infamous process losses referred to earlier in this book).

These assumptions are extremely strong and gratuitous. They are a poor fit, even when applied to the operation of the ubiquitous ad hoc laboratory groups for which they were more or less designed, and an even poorer fit when applied to real groups in natu-

ral settings. In contrast, TIP theory insists on treating the complexities of process that often are omitted in research on technology and
groups: that groups pursue multiple functions for multiple projects by means of complex time/activity paths.

These complexities are intricately related to the issues of information richness of media and information requirement of tasks
discussed earlier. TIP theory places emphasis on the importance of
developmental features of work groups. Some of the implications
for technology of those more complex developmental processes
suggested by TIP theory are discussed in Chapter 5.

CONCLUDING COMMENTS

The conceptual formulations outlined in this chapter provide an
array of interesting viewpoints from which to consider the effects
of technology on the flow of work in groups. They are to some
degree complementary, although heretofore they have not been
tightly interrelated within a single comprehensive formulation.
(Our formulations in this chapter, and those provided in Chapter
5, are an attempt to take some major steps in that direction). These
ideas provide a helpful guide both in our review of the empirical
research in this area and in our attempt to develop an integrated
theoretical treatment of groups. Results of that empirical review
are presented in the next chapter. Our attempt to provide a theoretical integration of the ideas presented here and the findings presented in the next chapter is laid out in Chapter 5, along with an
agenda for strategically crucial future research in this domain.

FOUR

Evidence: A Summary of Empirical Research Regarding the Effects of Electronic Technology in Work Groups

In Chapter 2 we presented a classification for the types of systems that have been developed to provide technological support for work groups; in Chapter 3 we presented a summary of theoretical formulations that add to an understanding of the effects of technology on work groups. This chapter reviews a much less richly articulated body of empirical evidence about such work groups. Although there is a very large volume of literature talking about uses of electronic technology to improve human performance, there is only a relatively small number of published reports that present systematic empirical evidence about the use of such technology in groups.

We carried out an extensive review of the literature, covering recent volumes of some 50 journals, and all of the books, technical reports, and research papers that we could locate. The appendix contains an annotated bibliography of that body of literature. We gathered all the bibliography we could find on our topic—the effects of technological support for work in groups—and ultimately cataloged over 250 articles. Of these, 51 articles presented (a) empirical evidence (b) about task performance of groups (c) that had some form of computer mediation. That data set turned out to encompass over 150 findings. A finding, here, is a (documented) assertion that there is (or isn't) an empirical relation between one or more independent and one or more dependent variables. A more detailed analysis of findings of that empirical literature is published elsewhere (Hollingshead & McGrath, in press).

Three other reviews of this literature have been published recently (Kraemer & King, 1988; Kraemer & Pinsonneault, 1990; McLeod, 1992), the latter a quantitative meta-analysis. Each of those specified a somewhat different topical focus, dealing with overlapping but not identical bodies of literature. Each of those reviews arrived at some of the same conclusions we did, but each also presents some differences in viewpoints, conclusions, and interpretations.

KEY VARIATIONS IN THE EMPIRICAL STUDIES

Even the relatively small set of empirical research studies presents a complex picture when one tries to aggregate and compare across studies. This research includes studies of groups of many different kinds, using electronic technology in many kinds of spatial and temporal patterns, doing many kinds of tasks, and operating under a range of system conditions. With such diversity, a simple additive aggregation of findings is not possible, nor would it be conceptually meaningful. We need to take at least three of those distinctions (spatial dispersion, temporal patterning, and task type) into account in our aggregation of findings, so that comparisons across studies can be interpreted sensibly. Those three distinctions are discussed briefly below.

Spatial Distribution of Group Members

Computer-mediated groups can be arrayed in at least three forms with respect to physical space. Some computer-mediated work involves groups whose members are all in the same room, and who can and do carry out some of their communication via oral communication and some of it via computer text. Other computer-mediated groups involve interaction of members who are in different places and therefore cannot make use of oral communication during meetings. Still other computer-mediated groups are in the same physical space but are precluded (either by instructions or by circumstances) from talking directly to one another. It can be argued that those latter groups are operating with a level of social presence or a mixture of social cues that is intermediate between groups that are physically separated and groups whose members can and do talk directly to one another.

Temporal Distribution of Group Activity

The literature in this area most often regards the temporal distinction as a simple dichotomy, distinguishing between groups working synchronously and those working asynchronously in time. The actual temporal distribution of group work presents a somewhat more complicated picture. For example: A set of coauthors who build a joint product over a matter of months might do a lot of their work via computer-mediated text messages but might nevertheless do some of their work in face-to-face meetings (or via other communication media such as phone or mail). Conversely, collaborators who are working primarily in direct, face-to-face mode may, from time to time, communicate with one another via electronic mail. In both cases, collaborators almost certainly will do a lot of the basic composition and editing of text off-line— that is, when working alone, not in interaction with collaborators by any medium of communication. There are at least three main temporal forms in which group work may be carried out:

I. *Single meeting:* A group may have only a single meeting, during which group members communicate (by direct or mediated means) primarily in an each-to-all fashion (with little or no each-to-some communication occurring during that meeting).

II. *A series of meetings:* A group may have a series of meetings, each held at a specific time, using some communication system, during which communication among members is primarily each-to-all. Members of such groups may or may not have each-to-some communication with other members between meetings, and if they do, it may or may not be by the same communication system used during meetings.

III. *A temporally distributed meeting:* A computer-mediated group can also take a third temporal form: A temporally distributed meeting in which members communicate each-to-all, via some computer-mediated communication system (e.g., e-mail), with members making their individual contributions in a temporally asynchronous pattern, distributed over a considerable period of calendar time. Such groups may or may not have additional each-to-some communications.

The theory underlying our work argues that, for the most part, groups are to be considered as continuing, intact social systems engaged in one or more relatively macroprojects, any one of which is likely to extend beyond the temporal boundaries of a single meeting (McGrath, 1990, 1991; see also Chapter 3). There may be some natural groups that do exist only for a single meeting and work on only a single topic, but by far the majority of natural groups have a life that extends beyond a single meeting on a single topic; thus the second temporal form is far more prevalent than the first.

Yet the research literature on work in computer-mediated groups is quite the opposite: By far the majority of studies of computer-mediated groups deal with single meetings of those groups. Often they deal with groups that exist only for a single meeting; a considerable portion of that literature deals with groups whose members are using that computer-mediated system for the first (and only) time.

The third temporal form reflects one of the major putative advantages of computers in group work, namely: Certain forms of electronic technology in work groups permit them to interact via computers, asynchronously, as in the use of bulletin board and e-mail technologies, to carry out collaborative work even when members do not work at the same time. Such asynchronous groups have neither a single meeting at a single period of time, nor multiple meetings at specified periods of time with distinct nonmeeting intervals between them; rather, the single meeting of such a group is itself distributed over an extended period of calendar time. Any one member is likely to be engaged with the group's business during some, but by no means all, of that time. In such a case, each member has considerable "between" times, during which he or she is not engaged in formal, each-to-all communication with the other members of the group via the computer-mediated system. Each-to-some communication among subsets of members of the group, by any of a range of media, may take place during these between times.

Variations in Task Type

Both natural work groups and those concocted for research purposes vary considerably in the kinds and level of difficulty of the tasks they are engaged in, but such differences are seldom adequately reflected in the research literature of the field. Ordinarily, studies involving natural groups use whatever specific task the extant groups do in their natural working environment. Most studies involving experimentally created work groups use an arbitrarily selected task of convenience. Neither of these approaches gives much attention to how task factors might alter the impact of the technology being studied. Yet on theoretical grounds (e.g., Daft & Lengel, 1986; McGrath & Hollingshead, 1993; see Chapter 3) there is reason to expect a strong interactive relation between task type and technology in affecting both group process and group task performance. The task circumplex model drawn from past work (McGrath, 1984; see Chapter 3) provides a classification schema that helped us take task type differences into account in our integration of research on technology in groups.

SOME METHODOLOGICAL ISSUES

Requirements for Generalizability
of Aggregated Findings

The logic of our approach implies that every empirical relation ultimately needs to be stated in terms of all of the variables relevant to the problem (see discussion and Figure 5.1 in Chapter 5). We take seriously the idea that empirical relations involving computer-aided groups should be regarded, at the outset, as probably a *joint* function of a number of group and member characteristics, task characteristics, and characteristics of the group's communication and task performance technology. All possible groups with different member compositions should not be expected to respond in the same way to a given technology; nor should technology be expected to have the same effects on groups doing different kinds of tasks or working with a communication and task performance technology that may vary in spatial, temporal, and many other features.

It is important to recognize also that the consideration of the effects of technology must be done with regard to some specific dependent variables, and that results are likely to depend on which dependent variables are examined. Not all parameters of performance, such as speed and quality, will vary in the same way and to the same degree in response to any given set of conditions; nor is task performance the only important outcome variable that may be affected by technology.

Given that point of view, meaningful empirical generalizations about the effects of, say, a computer-based synchronous communication system on task product quality, requires specifying at least:

How such relations vary with (or do not vary over) a number of group and member characteristics (e.g., Does group size matter? Are CEOs just like college students? and so on);

How such relationships vary with (or do not vary over) task types (e.g., Are brainstorming, decision, and planning tasks all affected in the same way and to the same degree by a given feature of the group's communication system?);

How such relations depend on (or do not depend on) the task structuring that accompanies the computer use.

Given that point of view, we can only make strong generalizations based on the empirical literature if that body of literature includes studies that vary, systematically: (a) important group and member characteristics, (b) task types and other task characteristics, and (c) communication media; and if at least some of those studies deal with the *same* set of dependent variables across such group, task, and media conditions.

Some Methodological Limitations
in This Body of Literature

The above is an ideal. However much we regard it as a methodological requirement, it is not a good description of very many bodies of literature in the behavioral and social sciences. It certainly is not a good description of the body of literature at hand.

Instead of those ideal conditions, the body of literature dealing with computer-assisted work in groups shows several serious limitations and confounds. First, the studies in this body of literature paid virtually no attention to any group or member characteristics (with the exception of a small number of studies that examined the effects of group size and technology on idea generation performance). Little is said about group composition, with respect to any characteristics (gender, task experience or competence, length of membership in the group, past experience with any computer or with this system being studied, and so on). Virtually nothing is said about group structure (e.g., Was there a division of labor? How did it get established?), although a few studies examined the effects of emergent and assigned leadership on groups interacting with technology. Very little attention is given to the specific populations of individuals who were participants in these studies. To aggregate findings across these studies would require us to regard studies with participants drawn from radically different populations (e.g., college students, company executives) as comparable. That is unlikely to be a useful assumption.

Moreover, the research to date has certainly not covered, systematically, the range of possible combinations of time and space dispersion and task type, as discussed above, nor compared electronic communication systems in various categories with face-to-face groups and with one another. There are relatively few studies within any one of the space/time combinations, and none at all in most of them. If differences in task types are considered, the body of literature is even more poorly distributed over categories.

Furthermore, and of considerable methodological importance, the body of literature as a whole suffers from a major confounding of several important facets. Almost all of the studies done by researchers trained in or working out of a given research locale or "lab" (e.g., Carnegie Mellon University, University of Minnesota, or University of Arizona) are likely to make use of:

1. the same spatial and temporal form of the technology;
2. the same type of research strategy (e.g., a lab experiment, or a case study strategy);
3. the same task type (e.g., brainstorming, or group decision), often using the same specific task within type (e.g., a group risky shift problem); and
4. a somewhat unique set of dependent variables (e.g., distribution of participation).

Together, these limitations and confounds add up to some serious impediments to generalization of findings. In the face of these several rather serious deficiencies we must summarize and interpret results with great caution.

*Methodological Considerations for a Single Study
Versus a Cumulative Body of Evidence*

Let us call attention at this point to a very important distinction that can easily get lost in a critical treatment of an aggregate body of literature such as the one presented here: The methodological criticisms given here, about confounds and so on, are *not* directed at the soundness of the methodology or conceptualization of any given study. Indeed, certain sets of studies within this body of literature are exemplary in that regard. In any case, most of the criticisms do not apply to individual studies but rather to aggregate bodies of work: the collective body of evidence about a given problem or issue.

The pursuit of scientific knowledge is, necessarily, a cumulative enterprise. Even if an entire literature is made up of methodologically and conceptually sound studies, it nevertheless can have serious limitations (confounds) when regarded as a whole. Such is the case here.

There is no reason why any one investigator ought to be expected to study all spatial and temporal patterns of use of technology in groups, or all task types shown in Figure 3.2, or all variables in any one of the panels of variables we have suggested as important, or even to measure all interesting and important dependent variables. Indeed, it is not possible to do so in any one study. There is no reason why any given investigator should try to cover that full range over a series of studies. Each study and each investigator's line of research must pursue its own purposes, and do so within many constraints of time, money, and other resources.

But those individual purposes, even vigorously pursued in sound methodological fashion by a number of researchers, can still leave the collective body of information seriously constrained, even flawed, so that it provides only a weak basis from which to generalize. There is no mechanism in science to channel individual research efforts in a way that will guarantee to maximize the information that can be gleaned from those efforts collectively. The scientific enterprise has no "invisible hand," no "market mechanism," to make everything come out for the best in the long run. If anything, the invisible hands (i.e., the underlying system forces) tend to press researchers toward doing good individual studies in ways that, in the long run, undercut the value of the collective body of knowledge (McGrath, Martin, & Kulka, 1982).

Nevertheless, to gain cumulative knowledge in any given field, researchers in that field must somehow find ways to generate a total body of empirical findings that permits sensible generalization across specific subissues. This matter is discussed again in the last chapter of this book.

TECHNOLOGY IN GROUPS: SUMMARY OF EMPIRICAL FINDINGS

The types of comparisons involved in the studies reviewed here, and the specific studies that fit each of those categories, are shown in Table 4.1. The studies themselves are summarized in the appendix; a detailed analysis of findings is given in Hollingshead and McGrath (in press). Here, we present a condensed summary only. The summary gives an indication of the range of dependent vari-

Table 4.1   Empirical Studies of Computer-Supported Groups

I. SINGLE MEETING

  A. Face-to-face vs. computer-supported groups (25 studies)

    1. GCSS (13 studies)

        Arunachalam (in press)
        Daly (1993)
        Dubrovsky, Kiesler, & Sethna (1991)
        Hiltz, Johnson, & Turoff (1986)
        Hiltz, Turoff, & Johnson (1988)
        Hollingshead (1993)
        Kiesler, Zubrow, Moses, & Geller (1985)
        McGuire, Kiesler, & Siegel (1987)
        Siegel, Dubrovsky, Kiesler, & McGuire (1986)
        Smith & Vanecek (1988)
        Smith & Vanecek (1990)
        Straus (1991)
        Weisband (1992)

    2. GPSS (12 studies)

        Gallupe, Bastianutti, & Cooper (1991)
        Gallupe, Dennis, Cooper, Valacich, Bastianutti, & Nunamaker (1992)
        Gallupe, DeSanctis, & Dickson (1988)
        George, Easton, Nunamaker, & Northcraft (1990)
        Ho & Raman (1991)
        McLeod & Liker (1992)
        Poole & DeSanctis (1992)
        Poole, Holmes, & DeSanctis (1991)
        Steeb & Johnston (1981)
        Valacich, Paranka, George, & Nunamaker (in press)
        Watson, DeSanctis, & Poole (1988)
        Zigurs, Poole, & DeSanctis (1988)

  B. Decision room groups (no face-to-face comparison) (13 studies)

        Adelman (1984)
        Connolly, Jessup, & Valacich (1989)
        Dennis, Heminger, Nunamaker, & Vogel (1990)
        DeSanctis, Poole, Lewis, & Desharnais (1991)
        Dickson, Lee, Robinson, & Heath (1989)
        Easton, George, Nunamaker, & Pendergast (1990)
        Jessup, Connolly, & Galegher (1990)
        Nunamaker, Vogel, Heminger, Martz, Grohowski, & McGoff (1989)

Table 4.1   (Continued)

B. (Continued)

   Sambamurthy, DeSanctis, & Poole (in press)
   Sambamurthy & Poole (in press)
   Valacich, Dennis, & Connolly (in press)
   Valacich, Dennis, & Nunamaker (1991b)
   Vogel & Nunamaker (1988)

C. Computer conference groups (no face-to-face comparison) (2 studies)

   Hiltz, Johnson, & Turoff (1991)
   Lea & Spears (1991)

D. Groups in decision room vs. dispersed (3 studies)

   Bui, Sivasankaran, Fijol, & Woodburg (1987)
   Gallupe & McKeen (1990)
   Jessup & Tansik (1991)

II. SERIES OF MEETINGS

   A. Face-to-face vs. computer (4 studies)

      1. GCSS

         Hollingshead, McGrath, & O'Connor (1993)
         Jarvenpaa, Rao, & Huber (1988)
         Walther & Burgoon (1992)

      2. GPSS

         Chidambaram, Bostrom, & Wynne (1991)

   B. Decision room groups (no face-to-face comparison) (1 study)

      Zigurs, DeSanctis, & Billingsley (1991)

III. EXTENDED TIME PERIOD

   A. Groups using computers vs. other media (e.g., phone, mail) (3 studies)

      1. Between-groups designs (1 study)
         Eveland & Bikson (1989)
      2. Within-groups designs (2 studies)
         Finholt, Sproull, & Kiesler (1990)
         Sproull & Kiesler (1986)

---

ables studied, and reflects the consistency or diversity of findings. The studies reviewed here fit into three main categories:

I. Studies of groups, with different communication media, for a single meeting
II. Studies of groups, with different communication media, for a series of meetings
III. Studies of groups using different communication media throughout an extended time period

Most of the research in our sample falls into the first of these categories: groups meeting at one time in one place. Most of that research is conducted in the laboratory with ad hoc groups. That research includes two main types: studies in which the computer provides a communication medium but by and large does not structure the task (GCSS); and studies in which the electronic system provides considerable task structure as well as a medium for communication (GPSS).

The second category, groups working together over a series of meetings, includes the two main types described in the previous category. The studies in this set involve the same groups working on different tasks (assigned by the researcher), each measured at a different point in time. These studies generally did not involve natural groups (i.e., groups that existed prior to and independent of the purposes of the researchers).

The third category, groups working throughout an extended time period, includes two types of studies: (a) between-groups studies that compare different groups working on a single project over a period of time, but that are using different communication media; and (b) within-group studies that examine each group's usage of various media over time and relate usage to other dependent variables. These studies generally involve a few natural groups that were carrying out tasks related to their own, rather than the researchers' purposes, with measures taken at several points in time.

Thus most of the research in our sample involved groups working on one task during one short meeting or an extended meeting over a period of time (30 studies). Twelve studies involved groups working on multiple tasks of the same task type during one meeting. Three studies involved groups working on multiple tasks of different task types during a single meeting. Only five studies involved groups working on multiple tasks of more than one task type over a series of meetings.

Five of the eight subtask types presented in McGrath's (1984) task circumplex are represented in this body of research (see also Chapter 3). Eleven studies employed an idea generation task. Twelve studies employed an intellective task in which group members searched for a demonstrable, correct answer. Sixteen studies employed a decision-making task in which groups had to reach consensus on a preferred answer. Five used cognitive conflict tasks in which group members had to resolve conflicts of viewpoints. Two studies used a mixed motive negotiation task where group members had to resolve conflicts of interest. In addition, seven studies used a task that incorporated multiple task types (e.g., idea generation and decision making). In five studies that were conducted with real groups, the group brought its own tasks to the group meeting. These studies generally were conducted in decision rooms with GPSS technologies. The tasks in one study were not described in enough detail to be classified.

The findings of these studies are summarized in the next section, one dependent variable at a time. The number of studies in which a given finding was obtained is indicated, and in many cases, the number of studies in which there was a finding in the opposite direction, or a finding of no difference, is also indicated. The findings are stated from the point of view of computer-aided groups, and except where otherwise specified, the comparison is with groups working face-to-face. That summary largely overlooks the confounding of results with respect to research strategy, task type, and dependent variables that was discussed previously, and overlooks, as well, the variations in group and member characteristics that have largely been ignored in this research area.

Note that the (unstated) modal finding for every dependent variable, over the 51 studies, is: "not tested." Even for distribution of participation over members, and decision time, which are the two most widely studied variables, more than half of the studies did not test them.

Interaction Process

Ten studies found the distribution of participation among members to be more equal with computer-supported groups, but four studies found no differences. One study found participation to be more equal with computer-supported groups in which status differences had been reduced. Several aspects of the amount and content of participation were studied: Computer groups had less overall participation in ten studies (no difference in two studies); more uninhibited communication in seven studies (no difference in three studies); more communication displaying positive affect in two studies; less argumentation in two studies; less social pressure in two studies, more of it in two studies, and no difference in five studies; more task-irrelevant communication in two studies, more task-relevant communication in three studies, and no differences in two studies; less socioemotional communication in two studies and more in one study; and less speculation in one study. Computer groups with anonymity had more critical communication in two studies, and more supportive communication in one study with no differences in one study.

Computer-supported groups had a higher degree of consensus in four studies. A facilitator or a designated leader improved the level of consensus in two studies and a higher level of support (Level 2 GDSS vs. Level 1 GDSS) improved consensus of computer groups in one study.

Computer-supported groups had a higher level of conflict than manual (that is, groups with nonelectronic decision support systems) groups in three studies. One study found that computer-supported groups managed conflict better, one found that manual groups managed conflict better, and one found that manual groups managed conflict better during the two initial sessions, but that computer-supported groups managed conflict better during the two final sessions.

Computer groups were less likely to have emergent leadership (two studies), but were more likely to have decentralized leadership (one study) and less stable leadership (one study). Computer-supported groups tended to de-emphasize personal relations and experience less interpersonal attraction (two studies.) However, one study found that computer-supported groups developed in a relationally positive direction over time and found no significant differences between computer and face-to-face groups. In one study, teams were more likely to use GPSS to aid in their group decisions when they were introduced to the technology early, rather than late, in their group development.

Task Performance

Groups using computers had longer task completion times (or decision times) in 12 studies (no difference in 1 study). Dispersed groups took longer in 1 study, shorter in another, compared to groups in a decision room.

Computer groups generated more solutions in 13 studies (no difference in 1 study); more task solution proposals (3 studies); more correct solutions in 1 study, but more errors (3 studies). Computer groups whose members were anonymous generated more solutions (3 studies), and computer groups who were instructed to be critical had more unique solutions (1 study). Larger computer groups generated more ideas per member than did smaller computer groups (5 studies).

Computer groups were less likely to reach consensus in two studies (no differences in three studies); computer groups with both a leader and feedback were less able to reach consensus than groups with either one of them (one study). Computer groups had more decision shift in three studies, with no differences in two studies.

Computer groups had better decision quality or performance in seven studies, had poorer performance in eight studies, and no differences in six studies. One study found that face-to-face groups performed better initially, but in a relatively short period of time (3 weeks), there were no significant differences for performance between face-to-face and computer-mediated groups. Manual groups had higher decision quality than GDSS, and both were higher than unstructured face-to-face groups (three studies). Computer-mediated groups were less likely to discuss the most important case attributes in two studies. Solutions were better for dispersed groups than decision room groups in one study, but there were no differences in another and decision quality was better for groups with more flexible (compared to less flexible) GDSS in one study.

Performance and task type. On idea generation tasks, computer-supported groups performed better than face-to-face groups in four studies (no difference in four studies). On intellective tasks, face-to-face groups performed better than computer groups in five studies, worse in one study, and no difference in one study. On decision-making tasks, computer groups performed better than face-to-face groups in two studies, worse in one study, and no difference in three studies. On negotiation tasks, face-to-face groups performed better than computer groups in two studies.

User Responses

Ratings of overall satisfaction were high for groups with computers in five studies (but these had no comparison groups, so the finding is not that they are higher than groups without computers). Computer groups had high ratings of satisfaction with process in two of those studies, high ratings of satisfaction with the system in two studies, and high satisfaction with outcome in one study.

In studies that did have comparison groups, computer groups had lower satisfaction with process in six studies, higher in four studies, with no differences in three studies; they also had lower satisfaction with outcome in two studies, higher satisfaction in one. Computer groups had lower satisfaction when the decision was structured than when it was unstructured (two studies).

Judgments of self and others were more negative in computer groups in three studies. User judgments of effectiveness were reported as high for computer groups in four studies that did not have comparison groups, but judgments of effectiveness were not different in two studies and were lower for computer groups in three studies that did have comparison groups.

Computer groups had a higher level of anxiety in one study, felt less freedom to participate in one study (no differences in one study), and were less accurate in their perceptions of the group interaction in one study. However, they perceived less evaluation apprehension (two studies) and less production blocking (two studies).

DISCUSSION

If this set of findings is regarded as the extant body of knowledge about these variables, and if we wish to interpret it optimistically (in an "overall weight of the evidence" manner), then we might draw the following cautious conclusions.

Amount of Interaction or Participation

Use of a computer-aided communication system (a GCSS) in a work group is likely to lead to a pattern of participation that overall is less in amount but more equally distributed among members. There apparently is more equal participation in computer-aided groups, although with some exceptions and with most studies simply not reporting on that variable. In virtually all cases, the equalization of participation occurs, because there is a great reduction in the total number of acts in computer-mediated as compared with face-to-face interactions. The computer does not simply reduce the participation of loquacious group members nor does it simply increase the participation of quiet group members.

All of these studies have ignored how group process is distributed over time (i.e., a problem-solving phase analysis), and over the group's functions, modes, and tasks. Those are the kinds of analyses called for by the group theory underlying our work.

In computer groups, there is less argumentation. On the other hand, in computer groups there may be more uninhibited communication, so-called flaming (especially in computer conferences), and more positive socioemotional communication. There seems to be more task relevant and irrelevant communication, and relatively more influence attempts. (Note: It is not clear how *all* of these participation results—increases in many categories but decreases in overall amount of communication—could be true at the same time. Perhaps the answer lies in the fact that most of the participation evidence is presented in terms of relative rates or proportions.) Computer systems may serve to surface conflict more effectively, although they may or may not have structuring procedures that help groups work through such conflict over time.

Group Task Performance

Groups with computers take longer to carry out a given task than do face-to-face groups (in spite of generating less participation or communication), at least on early task trials before group members have much experience with the technology. They are also less likely to reach consensus (but have a higher degree of consensus if they do reach consensus).

One group of findings show that computer groups tend to have higher-quality products on certain tasks (i.e., idea generation tasks), and another group of findings show that face-to-face groups tend to have higher-quality products on other tasks (i.e., intellective and negotiation tasks). Longitudinal research suggests that this relation may be attenuated over time. Several studies show that a manual version of the same task (with the high task structuring of GPSS but without electronic communication) gave even higher quality decisions than the GPSS with computer, which in turn were higher than the "no structure" face-to-face condition. This suggests that it may be the task structure rather than the computer mediation that influences decision quality on these tasks. The task structure may include procedures that simplify the handling of complex information; procedures that explicate agenda, thus making group process more organized; and procedures that expose conflict, and help the group to deal with it.

User Responses

Regarding user responses, one further distinction needs to be noted. When a comparison group is used (e.g., computer vs. face-to-face), results for satisfaction and user-rated effectiveness are equivocal, about evenly split among findings of higher, lower, and no difference for computer groups. When no comparison group is used, on the other hand (e.g., in studies using only groups in a decision room), researchers almost always find high levels of satisfaction and of user-rated effectiveness. Note that in almost all small group research, done in either laboratory or field settings with groups not using electronic technology, most participants report attitudes toward (i.e., satisfaction with) their groups relatively far toward the positive end of rating scales. To interpret responses of computer-assisted groups as high, without having a comparison with noncomputer group conditions, really may give us less information about user satisfaction with the technology at hand than about systematic biases in human respondents' use of rating scales. Note, too, that *effectiveness* has highly variable meanings in these user rating studies (including one study in which *effective* turns out to mean "more equal participation").

Users may or may not like using the computer, perhaps depending on their expectations prior to use of the system, their "stake in the game" (e.g., if they have already invested heavily in the system), previously existing norms in the group, and/or their own experience with the system. These reactions may or may not get more favorable over time.

CONCLUDING COMMENTS

It is apparent that any generalization one might make from these results is very shaky. Whereas each individual study may be methodologically strong and sound (many are, some are not!), the body of literature as a whole is burdened with a triple or quadruple confounding of communication system, task type, and research strategy. Furthermore, the literature virtually ignores all group and member variables. Finally, there is wide variation in dependent variables, and they tend to cluster within the confounded task-media-strategy clusters.

The vast majority of the research on which these conclusions are based is static; that is, it involves ad hoc groups using computer systems for a single session, often for the first and only time, compared with face-to-face groups (whose members have been using that "technology" all their lives). There is no reason to be confident that any of these findings, even those that are apparently robust over studies, will be robust over time and increased experience with the technology. Indeed, the findings of the few studies over time suggest that they will not. We address this question, and describe results of our recent work that bears on it, in the final chapter of the book.

As noted, to some extent this area currently has a half dozen or so separate bodies of evidence: separate sets of facts deriving from separate subbodies of work, done in different research settings, and dealing with different communication media, different tasks, and different dependent variables. *The problem is not that those sets of facts disagree; rather, it is that they cannot be compared, because they deal with different parts of the domain and do so in different research languages.* We address that issue, as well, in the final chapter.

FIVE

Integration and Agenda for Future Research

In earlier chapters we dealt with the systems, the ideas, and the evidence that make up the body of research about technology and groups. Here, we face the formidable tasks of trying to pull it all together into an integrative picture and laying out an agenda for future research.

The last section of Chapter 3 gives an outline of the basic group theory that has guided our work, stressing some of its implications for the study of technology in groups. In the first section of this chapter, we build on that group theory, and on the empirical evidence summarized in Chapter 4, in an attempt to formulate a model of the research problem—that is, an overall conceptual framework. That framework identifies key sets of variables pertinent to the phenomena involved in applications of technology to work groups, and suggests some patterns of relations among them. We then extend that framework to the dynamic case, examining some effects of continuity and change over time on key factors.

The third section of this chapter presents five main themes, each with several subthemes, that constitute an agenda of important issues for future research, and makes some suggestions about how the research community involved in the study of technology in groups could encourage the kind of integrative efforts we think are vital for effective development of a cumulative body of knowledge in this domain.

A CONCEPTUAL FRAMEWORK
FOR RESEARCH PLANNING

Research on the effects of technology on work in groups has largely ignored the ways in which effective work in groups is contingent on features of the group and its members, features of the task, and features of the situation (Hollingshead & McGrath, in press). Few effects are likely to hold across all possible systems and all uses; rather, the effects obtained in any given case will almost certainly be contingent on a host of factors. The impact of technology depends on the time and space distribution of the group's work, the nature and qualities of the tasks in which they are engaged, and the degree to which various portions of the group's work are prestructured, as well as on various characteristics of the group, its members, and its context.

Thus there are a plethora of potentially relevant factors, far too many to incorporate in any given study as design variables, or as factors to control statistically or experimentally. Furthermore, the logic of our guiding theoretical conceptions argues that the most important effects in this domain are likely to be interactive consequences of the joint operation of a number of variables, rather than main effects of differences in one. For example: It is unlikely that computer-mediated groups will be superior to face-to-face groups for all tasks and in all circumstances, and equally unlikely that they will be inferior on all tasks and in all circumstances. It is far more likely that communication media and task will interact with each other, and with other factors as well, so that the proper question has to do with the set of conditions under which one or another technology will yield best results.

Therefore, it is useful to construct a workable conceptual framework, or a model of the research problem at hand: a framework that encompasses the full panoply of potentially relevant variables and places them in functional relation to one another. Such a

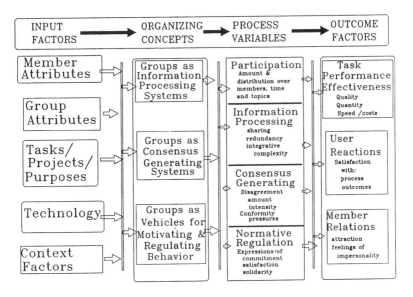

| INPUT FACTORS | ORGANIZING CONCEPTS | PROCESS VARIABLES | OUTCOME FACTORS |

Figure 5.1. A Conceptual Framework for Studying the Impact of Technology on Groups

framework can provide a useful guide for research planning. It can help formulate strategic theoretical hypotheses about these issues, construct sound empirical studies to test those hypotheses, and provide a rationale that will help relate empirical results across studies.

Such a framework is presented in Figure 5.1. It construes the research problem in terms of a sequence of four panels of variables. The first panel consists of five classes of input factors that form the basic constituents of work groups in context: member attributes, group attributes, variables related to task/project/purposes, variables related to communication and task performance systems (or, more generally, technology), and variables in the group's physical, social, and temporal context. These fill the methodological function of independent variables.

The second panel is a set of ways to conceptualize the operation of groups: organizing concepts that are, in effect, metaphors for the functions served by work groups. These organizing concepts, and the sets of variables they subsume, function as bases for interpretation of how combinations of input factors lead to changes in process and outcome variables.

Next is a set of indices that reflect the patterns of activity that occur while the group is doing its work. Methodologically, these are process variables. For some purposes they can be regarded as dependent variables (i.e., consequences of input conditions as mediated by intervening variables). For other purposes they can be regarded as independent variables (i.e., as bases for the levels and patterns of outcome variables; see following).

Finally, there is a set of variables that reflect subsequent conditions—for the group, for its task, and for its members—that result from the group's work. Methodologically, these outcome factors are explicit or implicit criteria for evaluation of the effectiveness of the group as a performance system.

The entries in these panels of variables in Figure 5.1 are intended to be illustrative, not exhaustive. They are drawn both from the group research literature and from the literature on computer-mediated task performance. Some of them were discussed in earlier chapters.

What we would like to be able to build, here, is a systematic map of all the empirical information that is available about all of the effects of all of the variables of each of these classes, and all of the theoretical information that is available about the conceptual meanings and implications of these postulated or observed effects. Such a map would constitute both an integration of research knowledge and a detailed agenda for subsequent research. Unfortunately, the state of the art in this area of study is far from the level of development that would permit such a strong mapping. What we must settle for, instead, is a very limited approximation of such an empirical and theoretical map. We offer discussion in the remainder of this section that we hope will aid in that mapping task, working through the four panels of Figure 5.1 from right to left, from outcome factors, to process variables, to organizing concepts, to input factors.

Outcome Factors: Multiple Criteria
of System Effectiveness

There are at least three standpoints from which one can assess the consequences of introduction of any given technology in work groups: task performance effectiveness, group interaction and performance processes, and user reactions to the system and its results. Ultimately, the value of such technology for enhancing the work of groups depends on its evaluation from all three of these standpoints. Thus assessment of the effectiveness of a technology of a work group should include (a) evidence of its direct impact on task performance, in use as well as during experimental trials; (b) evidence of its effects on crucial group interaction and performance processes, which in turn may have longer-term effects on group task performance; and (c) evidence of its impact on system users, including the degree to which the system is judged effective and usable by the groups (and individuals) who will use the technology, and by higher levels in the embedding organizational systems within which that work is taking place. Each of these, in turn, constitutes a panel of criterion variables rather than a single criterion attribute. (For example, task performance effectiveness needs to be reckoned in terms of quality, quantity, and cost.) These three panels of criteria are discussed next.

Indices of Task Performance Effectiveness

We (and others) have used the term *group task performance effectiveness* as if it were a single variable; instead, that notion incorporates a number of important variables—parameters of performance—not all of which are positively correlated with one another across groups, tasks, and circumstances. For example, performance must be reckoned in terms of quantity, quality, and cost (of which speed, or cost in time, is a special case). Those three are a system of variables having to do with effectiveness: a system not unlike temperature, volume, and pressure of a gas, for which there are two rather than three degrees of freedom. A given communication system, task, or group property often affects one of those parameters adversely and another favorably. For example, certain forms of group decision support systems are posited as increasing at least some aspects of decision quality at least under some conditions (of member, group, task, and context). But groups virtually always take longer to reach consensus, and to carry out the task, using such support systems. Furthermore, there are often multiple criteria for assessing each of these—that is, more than one conception of quality, or of quantity, or of cost. For example, for many idea generation tasks it is important to consider both the originality or creativity of the ideas and their practicality or feasibility; there is considerable evidence that those attributes often correlate negatively, and seldom correlate positively, for a given task.

Measures of User Reactions

A full assessment of the impact of technology (or any other major feature of groups in context) ought to take into account the impact of its use on the users. It is a truism in organizational lore that strong belief by users that a given new technology is not effective is virtually a self-fulfilling prophecy (although an equally strong belief that it is effective may be less self-fulfilling). Assessment ought to deal with a series of user reactions: member satisfaction with the group, the task, the group's task performance, and the communication medium being used; (changes in) interpersonal attraction to the other members of the group; evaluation of the difficulty, complexity, interest, and importance of the task; and so forth.

Moreover, the members of the work group themselves are not the only people who have a stake in the success of a given technology, and whose satisfaction with the technology will affect the long-run success of the system. Other important stakeholders may include other personnel in the organization who are affected by the work group's process and performance; personnel in and outside the group whose value to the organization may change depending on the success of the technology; segments of the organization that will bear the costs of the new system, and that will carry responsibility for its success; and clients and customers whose goods and services will be affected by the success of the work group and its technology. The interests of these various stakeholders are often in conflict or competition, rather than in accord, with one another. Hence assessment of user reactions to a new technology requires a complex set of information, even before it is combined with performance (and process) evaluations.

Process Variables: Results of Inputs and Causes of Outcomes

Group process variables stand in a methodologically special position in our interpretation of the research problem: On one hand, they are dependent variables vis-à-vis the input factors; that is, variables of the several classes of input factors, separately and in combination, all are potential contributors to shaping group interaction process. On the other hand, process variables are independent variables vis-à-vis task performance outcomes. Most group theory and research assumes that group interaction processes are an important basis by which group task performance is shaped. The empirical evidence for such process/outcome relations is limited and mixed.

We need to specify a set of variables that reflect the major variations in group interaction processes relevant to the impact of technology on groups, and then gather information about how those variables are affected by various input factors and how those effects get reflected in group task performance. That means that we need to have a map of the theoretically postulated and empirically established relations both between input factors and process, and between process and task performance and other outcome factors. The latter represents a crucial part of our specification of criteria of group task performance effectiveness.

Some of these technology/process relations have been addressed, notably in the research of Kiesler and colleagues (see chapters 3 and 4). For example, they have studied the impact of technology (via the intervening variables of anonymity, loss of social cues, and depersonalization) on participation of low-status members in group discussions. Much more of such research is needed, and should be carried out in a comprehensive, systematic, and temporally extended programmatic fashion.

Furthermore, such research needs to address a related set of issues: To what extent, and in what patterns, are these process variables related to relevant outcome measures? For example, much of the research assessing the effects of technology on distribution of participation among members has worked on the assumption that equal participation of all group members was an unmixed blessing, both for task performance effectiveness and for user reactions. But there are often situations in which equal participation by all group members may decrease the efficiency and effectiveness of the group on its task, and/or decrease satisfaction of many of the members with the group and its work, because group members have unequal expertise and knowledge to contribute to a given task, and there is not necessarily a high positive correlation between members' willingness to contribute and the value of those contributions to the group.

There are similar issues about the relation between such aspects of process as information sharing, normative versus informational influence, integrative complexity of arguments, and so on. When information is distributed in a group, the issue of what and how much information to share, and how to do so, poses a dilemma for group members, namely: Total sharing of all information by all members can produce massive information overload; yet withholding of crucial information by some members can produce ineffective task performance and can breed intragroup distrust.

Thus the issue of the relation of group process variables to task and user consequences is neither trivial nor simple. It needs to be fully explored in future research to unscramble some of the *why* as well as the *what* of effects of technology on groups. (Some of these process issues will be discussed, as substantive topics, later in this chapter.)

Concluding Comments About Criteria

In past research, a number of variables from each of these criterion panels have been studied, but different studies have emphasized different subsets of them. Some researchers have studied amount of productivity; others have assessed quality of decisions. Still others have focused on member participation patterns, or on user reactions. It is vital that research in an area of study be cumulative, that later studies can build on earlier ones so that their findings can be compared. It is necessary, therefore, that successive studies make use of the same, or at least of overlapping, sets of dependent variables for evaluating system outcomes.

The solution to this problem involves more than just using more dependent variables in studies. Ultimately, this area of inquiry will need to build a thorough and systematic criterion system: a conceptual schema that deals with questions of the weight or importance to be assigned to those three standpoints, and to the various criterion attributes within each panel, in order to have an adequate evaluation of the impact of (various kinds of) technology on (various kinds of) groups.

Organizing Concepts: Multiple
Interpretations of Group Functions

Figure 5.1 lists alternative organizing concepts by which researchers can interpret effects. These concepts, and the pattern of the factors subsumed under them, are ostensibly summaries or reflections of the combination of input conditions that prevails in any given case; they are also presumably descriptions of factors affecting subsequent group process and outcomes. We suggest that there are at least three useful sets of such organizing concepts, that those three sets of concepts can be construed as three metaphors for the group's main function(s), and that those three sets of concepts bear a complex relation to the functions specified in TIP theory (see Figure 3.1):

Groups as information-processing systems: This pertains primarily to the production function.

Groups as consensus-generating and conflict-resolving systems: This pertains primarily to the group well-being function.

Groups as vehicles for motivating and regulating member behavior: This pertains primarily to the member support function.

These three metaphors, and some issues associated with each of them, are discussed next.

Groups as Information-Processing Systems

Researchers and scholars working with groups have construed them in terms of many different metaphors: all the way from the discredited group mind and group consciousness concepts, to Lewin's "field of forces," the dramaturgical metaphor of Moreno's work, the hydraulic system metaphor implicit in Freud's work, the machine metaphor implicit in Frederick Taylor's time and motion approach, and the living organism metaphor implicit in much of the group dynamics movement and of systems theory. One metaphor conspicuously absent in earlier decades but now gaining prominence—paralleling developments in other parts of psychology and the behavioral and social sciences—is the metaphor of groups as information-processing systems. This conceptualization seems especially appropriate for the study of effects of technology (largely information-handling technology) on work in groups. Three promising lines of work can be identified within this theme.

The first of these has to do with the effects of technology on information-processing patterns in groups. Here, the work of Malone (1988) is prominent, and can be extended to deal with technology. In this domain, also, is some of the work on group heuristics and other aspects of information processing at a group level. Another line of research in this domain has to do with the joint effects of technology, patterns of information distribution, and information sharing on work in groups. Here, the work of Gary Stasser and colleagues stands out (e.g., Stasser & Stewart, 1992). There is ongoing work on effects of technology on information sharing by Hollingshead (1993).

A third line of research related to groups as information-processing systems is work by Wegner and colleagues (Wegner, 1986) on development and use of transactive memory in groups. This work views groups as information-processing systems with information distributed over a multiperson transactive memory, bringing in standard cognitive issues of information encoding, processing, storage, retrieval from memory, and so on. It also deals with the not so standard notions that incoming information may get allocated to one or another person, and be encoded only by that person, and that others must encode, store, and be able to retrieve a "table of contents" reflecting where various kinds of information are likely to be stored. This work also needs to consider the critical dependence of such a distributed cognitive system (a transactive memory) on continuity of membership in the group. This is one important reason for studying effects of changes in membership, an issue reflected in Theme IV (discussed later in this chapter) dealing with change over time. There is work on other aspects of group memory and related issues by Verlin Hinsz, by Scott Tinsdale, by David Vollrath, and by others.

All three of these lines of research regarding groups as information-processing systems fit together into a broader research theme referred to in the work of John Levine and colleagues (Levine & Moreland, 1991; Levine, Resnick, & Higgins, 1993) as "socially shared cognitions" or as a "sociocognitive" approach to groups (see, also, Gruenfeld & Hollingshead, 1993). This, we think, is an extremely promising area for future study of groups, with and without technology.

Groups as Consensus-Generating Systems

Another way in which one can conceptualize the function of groups is as vehicles for the development of consensus and the resolution of conflict among contending interests and values; that is, groups as vehicles for carrying out political, as distinguished from cognitive, work. Research on group problem solving, in general, has given far too little attention to conflict and to the operation of such political processes in groups. When they have been introduced in group research, it has usually been as potential sources of group task performance errors (e.g., Steiner's concept of process losses), as symptoms of deficiencies in group decision making (e.g., Janis's "groupthink" and related conceptions), or as problematic features of bargaining and negotiation tasks. Seldom have they been considered as normal and indeed desirable aspects of group work. Yet researchers who have been concerned with the implementation process (see discussions in Chapter 3) recognize such political activities as essential to the effective adoption of rational systems. These are not really separate from the rational, information-processing aspects of groups, but it is worth stressing their distinctiveness because they have too often been overlooked in research on group task performance.

Groups as Systems for Motivating and Regulating Behavior

Still another way to regard the function of groups is as vehicles for the operation of social influence processes among members of a collectivity. This includes concern with how technology alters the space and time constraints on who can interact, making possible the formation of groups quite unlike any we have seen before (e.g., groups who interact regularly and densely but have never seen one another). Kiesler and Sproull discuss this aspect of technology. These possibilities do carry some constraints, too; for example, those members know each other in some respects but do not know each other in some other crucial ways. This domain also includes concern with the effects that technology has on the norms and practices by which group members communicate with one another: rates and timing of participation, distribution of participation among members and among content categories, task focus of interaction, minimization of certain kinds of emotional or interpersonal expression, and yet the startling outbursts of highly emotional flaming and negative criticisms. All of these deserve much more comprehensive research than they have been given to date.

Input Factors: Determinants of Group Task Performance

Group performance of any task is a joint function of a relatively large number of variables of each of several sources or classes (the five sets of input conditions). An account needs to be built of what is known (and of what yet needs to be found out through empirical research) regarding the separate and combined effects of every one of these potentially important input conditions. All of the input variables can be represented in terms of the five main classes, singly and in intersecting pairs:

1. Member characteristics: Properties of the individual users (cognitive, affective, conative, and demographic) who, presumably, are members of groups.
2. Group characteristics: Properties of the group qua group, both compositional (e.g., heterogeneity of members on one or more specific characteristics) and structural (e.g., degree of status hierarchy).
3. Task characteristics: Properties of the task/project/activities in which the group is engaged.
4. Technology characteristics: Properties of any technological systems (both hardware and software) used in the group for communication, for information input, and for task support.
5. Context characteristics: Properties of the context: physical (e.g., noise, heat); sociocultural (e.g., general cultural norms); and temporal (e.g., deadlines, weekends, seasons).

In addition to these five basic classes of input variables, there are sets of variables that lie at the intersection of each pair of these classes. Thus, for example, some variables are a joint function of group members and task, such as degree of task experience, rather than being a property of either one of them alone. Potentially, the intersections of all pairs of these classes contain such important joint variables. Thus there are:

Member-Group variables (e.g., tenure of member within the group)
Member-Task variables (e.g., task experience)
Member-Technology variables (e.g., computer experience or attitudes)
Member-Context variables (e.g., member status in the organization or in the embedding culture)
Group-Task variables (e.g., coordination requirements of the group for task completion)
Group-Technology variables (e.g., relation of the group's size to system capacity)
Group-Context variables (e.g., organizational status of group)
Task-Technology variables (e.g., fit of information richness needs and opportunities)
Task-Context variables (e.g., task deadlines)

Technology-Context variables (e.g., organizational norms regarding use of computer systems)

There are of course many important three-way contingencies among variables of these various input classes. For instance, there are Group-Task-Technology interactions (e.g., the extent and difficulty of coordination requirements imposed on the group for performance of a task of a given type may depend on the technology being used). We will not extend this list of possibilities to completion here. Our main point is that there is a plethora of variables involving these classes of input factors, singly and in combination, that need to be studied.

This classification schema thus poses 5 single and 10 joint classes of variables as major sources of effects, and suggests additional combinations of 3 or more classes. Each of those classes of variables contains a number of subclasses, and each of them includes many individual variables.

From even a cursory examination of the research literature on the effects of technology on work in groups, it is obvious that few of these variables have been studied systematically, and many of them have not been studied at all. We can say virtually nothing, for example, about the effect of attributes of the system users (group member characteristics), or about the effects of any properties of the groups using the system (group composition or structure); nor can we say much about effects of various aspects of the task, or of task-member joint effects.

A full discussion of all important variables of all of these classes of factors is far beyond the scope of this book (and, indeed, beyond the present state of the art in this domain). In the following pages we discuss certain of these classes of variables, focusing on those we regard as having been especially understudied, relative to their conceptual and empirical importance.

Member and Group Attributes

There is a vast body of research literature on the effects of features of the group and its members—features traditionally referred to in group research as individual characteristics, group composition, and group structure (for summaries, see McGrath, 1984;

Moreland & Levine, 1992). But for the most part that body of work has been ignored in research dealing with technology. Research that does not reckon with groups as continuing, purposive, multi-functioned, and to some degree particularized, interactive social systems is unlikely to help much in developing and applying technology to improve work in real-life groups. Whereas some of the best work in this domain does treat groups from such a complex and dynamic perspective, most of the work in this area does not.

There are several ways in which member and group characteristics can be viewed. There are a variety of attributes of group members that may affect how a given group and its members are likely to behave in a group context, and how that behavior is likely to translate into task performance outcomes. These variables can be considered both as individual attributes, for which the level of the variables may be important (e.g., the level of task expertise), and as features of group composition, for which the homogeneity/heterogeneity of the group may be crucial (e.g., a group in which members have relatively equal levels of status in the organization may be more effective for tasks requiring coordination). These include factors indicative of individual status and cultural background, factors reflecting individual experience and ability on the task, and factors indicating individual attitudes and values (e.g., age, gender, task ability, task experience, group/organizational seniority and experience, education, socioeconomic/racial/ethnic background, and attitudes toward the task, the group, the organization).

In addition to such individual member attributes, some features of the group qua group are also important. Group size is important with respect to many aspects of process and performance. Furthermore, groups often are structured (perhaps along status or authority lines) in ways that affect group process, hence group outcomes.

Obviously, this category includes a very large number of variables that are potentially important in use of technology in groups—far more than can be incorporated into any given study as design variables, or as factors to be controlled statistically or experimentally. Yet those variables cannot be ignored if systematic knowledge in this domain is to be developed.

Group-Technology and Group-Task Interactions

Besides features of individual members, and attributes of the group as a group, there also are potentially important contingency effects that pertain to groups and their technology, on the one hand, and groups and their tasks on the other. (We will discuss the very important task-technology interaction in the next section.) For example: All groups have a history, carried in memory by its members; but this history often varies from member to member in what is remembered and how that information is interpreted. Part of that history entails the group's experience with the particular tasks and/or technologies: the group's level of experience, and its past success or failure with that technology or on that task, members' attitudes toward that technology or that task, and so on. All of these can moderate the effects of a given technology.

Task-Technology Fit

We have already suggested that research on technology and groups also needs to pay more attention to features of the task(s) that those groups are to carry out. To some degree, the modules of every GPSS explicitly or implicitly reflect the categories of a crude typology of tasks or of task processes: idea generation, proposal evaluation, alternative selection, consensus seeking, and the like.

Earlier work (McGrath, 1984) presented a classification system for distinguishing different types of group tasks and relating them to one another (see Chapter 3 and Figure 3.2). That task circumplex model posits four basic task performance processes, each with two major subtypes: to generate (ideas or plans); to choose (a correct answer or a preferred answer); to resolve (conflicting views or conflicting interests); and to execute (in contests against another group(s) or in competition with external standards of performance). Those four processes (or eight task types) are related to one another as the quadrants (octants) of a circumplex structure. The two dimensions defining the space of that circumplex are (a) the kind and degree of interdependence among members in the task performance process (from coaction or collaboration, to cooperation or coordination, to conflict or competition); and (b) the degree to which the processes involve cognitive versus behavioral activities (see Figure 3.2). Here, we are interested primarily in the cognitive hemisphere of that circumplex.

Some GPSS (e.g., DeSanctis & Gallupe, 1987; Zigurs et al., 1988) explicitly use that task circumplex as a model from which to derive their list of modules; other systems (e.g., Nunamaker, Dennis, Valacich, Vogel, & George, 1991) use terms and distinctions quite compatible with it. We therefore will take that circumplex schema as a useful initial guide for the present context, and will draw on it below.

In recent work in our research program, we have hypothesized that one axis of that circumplex space orders the task types along a dimension similar to Daft and Lengel's (1986; Trevino, Lengel, & Daft, 1987) "information richness" concept. As discussed in Chapter 3, Daft and Lengel posit that group tasks differ in how much they require the transmission of information that is more or less "rich" in its contents. To oversimplify: Richness of information refers to how much the information contains "surplus" emotional, attitudinal, normative, and other meanings, beyond the literal cognitive denotations of the symbols used to express it. Presence of redundant information, perhaps via nonverbal and paraverbal channels, also adds to the richness of the information transmitted and provides bases for reducing its equivocality. Tasks requiring groups to generate ideas (e.g., simple brainstorming tasks) may require only the transmission of specific ideas; evaluative and emotional connotations about message and source are not required and are often considered to be a hindrance.

On the other hand, tasks requiring groups to negotiate and resolve conflicts of views or interests may require the transmission of maximally rich information, including not only facts, but also values, attitudes, affective messages, expectations, commitments, and so on. Tasks requiring groups to solve intellective problems (problems that have correct answers) lie in between the two extremes noted above, but nearer the low richness end; whereas tasks requiring groups to reach decisions on issues for which there is not a right answer, but only a consensus (such as a jury verdict or a policy choice) lie in between the two extremes but nearer the high richness end.

Daft and colleagues (Daft & Lengel, 1986; Trevino et al., 1987) maintain (and we agree) that communication media differ in the richness of the information that they can and do convey. Face-to-face communication among interpersonally involved humans is the richest medium; communications in standardized written form among strangers may be the least rich. The electronic media in general, and computer communication in particular, are well toward the low-richness end of that continuum, compared with face-to-face communication.

Daft and colleagues argue that the effectiveness of a system on a task will vary with the fit between the richness of information that can be transmitted via that system's technology and the information richness requirements of that system's tasks. By that hypothesis, it is likely that groups with electronic technology (compared with face-to-face groups) will yield effective task performance if they are doing tasks at or near the "generate" (low richness) pole of the circumplex, but will be very ineffective for tasks at or near the "negotiate" pole of that space. That hypothesis ought to apply to the use of electronic GCSS for tasks of various types, as well as to the use of electronic GPSS for performance modules of various types; insofar as activities in either of those cases entail use of electronic GISS, it should hold for that category of support systems as well.

The pattern of relations reflected in the Daft-Lengel hypothesis, as we have applied it to the domain of group support systems, is shown systematically in Figure 5.2. This figure presents a four-by-four space defined in terms of the four task types on the cognitive hemisphere of the circumplex (see Figure 3.2), and the four media forms discussed in relation to GCSS (see Figure 2.1). This figure identifies patterns of differential fit between (a) the information richness requirements of the tasks in which groups might be engaged and (b) the information richness potential of the communication media that such groups might use.

The best fitting combinations of information richness of task and media lie near the main diagonal of the space. Contours successively distant from that diagonal represent successively less well-fitting combinations—for different reasons on the two different halves of the space. Task-technology combinations that depart

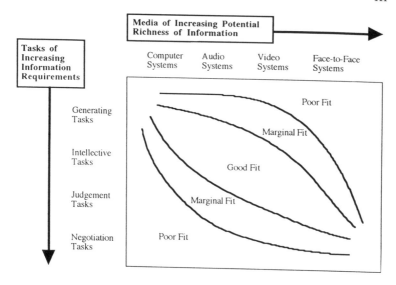

Figure 5.2. Task-Media Fit on Information Richness
NOTE: See also McGrath and Hollingshead (1993).

from the best fit diagonal in the northeast direction (i.e., the technology provides more richness of information than the tasks require) are poor fits only with regard to efficiency. Those groups can do their tasks effectively within the constraints of their communication media; but they also can engage in information exchanges involving much more richness and surplus meaning than the tasks demand. Hence such groups are always vulnerable to inefficiency brought about by the distraction of communications that are nonessential for effective task performance. However, this matter can be viewed more optimistically from a group-theoretic perspective (see discussion of effects over time later in this chapter).

On the other half of the space, task-technology combinations that depart from the best fit diagonal in the southwest direction—that is, cells with tasks that require more richness than their technology can deliver—are vulnerable not to problems of efficiency but to problems of effectiveness and quality of performance. Members of groups in those situations not only are not distracted by potential exchanges of too rich information with surplus meanings; they have communication media that are not capable of transmitting information sufficiently rich to let them carry out the high-richness demands of their tasks (i.e., to let them reduce the high equivocality in the situation). But this, too, can be viewed more optimistically from a group-theoretic perspective (see discussion of effects over time later in this chapter). Note, also, that the difference between the two halves of the space reflects the efficiency versus flexibility (effectiveness) trade-off that Malone (1988) emphasizes (see Chapter 3).

To some degree, however, the information richness of a medium inheres in the social processes by which it is put to use. That, in turn, depends on the development of communication norms whereby the collaborators establish agreed-on extradenotative meanings by which they can insert some useful richness into a particular medium (e.g., use of caps, brackets, or asterisks to denote emphasis in e-mail messages). Recently completed research in our program (Straus, 1991) confirms the potential importance of the task-by-technology interaction.

CONTINUITY AND CHANGE OVER TIME: A DYNAMIC FRAMEWORK

We noted earlier that, in addition to effects of these various classes of input factors, and their interactions two at a time, there are some important contingencies among them of an even more complex nature. One particular set of these more complex contingencies are those that interact with time; that is, effects of input factors that shift as groups develop and gain experience with given tasks and technologies. We will discuss some of those temporal or change effects here.

Changes in the Impact of Technology With Increased Experience

In a recently completed longitudinal study, a set of computer groups and a parallel set of face-to-face groups worked on a variety of tasks over an extended period of time, remaining as intact groups with the same technology throughout much of that period (Hollingshead et al., 1993).

The impact of technology on task performance was expected to be affected by task type, and in particular by the extent to which tasks require that individual performances fit together into a group product (i.e., require coordination and consensus). There were such task-technology effects, but less strongly than anticipated. In contrast, effects of experience with the technology were very strong. A technology new to the participants appears, initially, to impede fast and efficient performance on various tasks; but those initial effects disappeared within about three once-a-week 2-hour sessions. Furthermore, when already established face-to-face groups were shifted to a new technology about 6 weeks into the experiment, they suffered similar reductions of performance speed and efficiency, but regained their prior performance levels when returned to their familiar face-to-face medium.

Group Development and Changes
in Task-Technology Fit

TIP theory hypothesizes that, if a group is performing only the production function for a single, simple, familiar task that has low information richness requirements, then the group will be likely to adopt a default time/activity path that is efficient (from the point of view of a researcher/observer working on the set of constraining assumptions noted earlier in relation to the concept of process losses). But when there are major changes in features of the task (e.g., increased task difficulty), features of the group (e.g., new group members), or features of the situation (e.g., changes in time limits), that group is faced with a more complex situation. In such a case, the efficient path is likely to show some perturbations. The group may need to engage in activities related to Modes II and III of the production function (i.e., technical problem solving and conflict resolution), and/or in activities related to any of the modes of the group well-being and member support functions. If so, then the group will need to carry on communications that require relatively rich information exchanges; that is, the group will move downward in the space shown in Figure 5.2. Thus, even if a group begins with an apparently simple task that fits an information-lean medium, increased complexities of group, task, and situation may lead them to migrate southward, into a region on the task requirements dimension for which their communication medium is no longer adequate.

Conversely, groups in early stages of their own development often may require relatively high levels of information richness in order to carry out their well-being and member support functions and to establish their task performance strategies. As those groups mature, however, they are likely to become able to carry out all of their functions, at least for routine projects, with much less rich information exchanges. As groups mature, one might say, they tend to migrate northward, into a region of the space requiring less rich information media.

Two additional complexities with respect to the task-technology fit need to be noted here. First, most of the discussion of these issues, in the literature of the field as well as in this book, presupposes that a given task is to be done using only one or another medium. The question of the effectiveness with which various communication media can be combined with one another is virtually unexamined in the literature of this area to date.

Second, the question of task-technology fit can be viewed with respect to whether a given technology contains a tool (a module) for any particular task that a group might have to do. For example, a given GPSS might contain a brainstorming module but not a policy analysis module, and a specific group on a specific occasion might need either, both, or neither of these tools. This issue can be stated more generally as having to do with the versatility of a given technology, and the range or flexibility of use of its modules (e.g., can a given brainstorming module be adapted to generate feasible and low-cost, rather than creative alternatives?). These issues, too, have not been considered very extensively in the research literature of this field, and their full consideration would seem to require development of something akin to a "theory of tasks" for the kinds of groups to be served by such technologies.

Thus the role of technology in the effective functioning of work groups is much more complex than our simplified research paradigms have taken into account. Furthermore, that role is dynamic, shifting over time as a function of the group's own history and its changing circumstances. For these systems to be studied systematically and used effectively in real-life contexts, these complexities of group process must be taken into account in research and in applications.

Learning and Adaptation for Members, Groups, and Organizations

One of the most prominent and important themes in the literature of this field is that both technologies and groups change when they are brought together in a particular context. Technology as implemented is seldom isomorphic with technology as designed. The group that uses such technology is itself changed in the process. That central proposition informs at least three lines of research prominent in this area:

1. Adaptive structuration: work by Poole and others that focuses on the interplay between how the group modifies the technology-as-offered, in order to make it work within the group, and how that process modifies the group itself (see Chapter 3).
2. Implementation: work by Bikson and others that focuses on the ways in which organizational-level policies affect how a given technology is brought into and put to use within that organization or its subdivisions (see Chapter 3).
3. Organizational learning: work by Argote and others that focuses not on the initial mutual adaptation of technology and group, as do the first two, but rather on how (and where) the group embeds the changes that come about as consequences of the experience of that group using that technology to accomplish its tasks: changes in group member skills and memories, in group norms, in the technology's hardware and software, and in the procedures by which the group applies that hardware. (For a summary, see Argote & McGrath, 1993.)

All of these lines of research seem productive and promising.

Changes in Membership, Tasks, and Technology

One of the most striking anomalies in group research, including research on technology in groups, has to do with constancy or variability of group membership. Group research projects usually take great pains to insure that the groups being studied have constant membership. This is often made easy because they are studying a given group for only a very short time, such as 1 or 2 hours. Naturally occurring groups, on the other hand, are strongly characterized by variations in membership—both temporary fluctuations from occasion to occasion, and permanent losses and gains of membership over relatively short segments of the group's entire life.

The purpose of holding group membership constant in research is to increase rigor: The groups are more comparable to one another, and a group's reactions to early and later events are likewise more comparable. But that strategy places serious limitations on the research information that can be garnered with it, insofar as natural groups ordinarily have fluctuations in membership and insofar as any of the group interaction and performance phenomena under study are substantially affected by such variations.

It is apparent from what has already been discussed that, on theoretical grounds, many key factors are likely to be very sensitive to which people are in fact present and active members of a given group on a given occasion. Among the potential effects of membership changes are decreases in group learning; disruptions in the development and use of transactive memory; increase in attention to group well-being and member support functions (e.g., division of labor, task roles); decrease in commitment to the group and its activities; and decrease in synchronization/coordination among members. There is remarkably little empirical evidence about such effects, however, and this surely is an area in which further research is needed.

All that has been said about the likely consequences of changes in group membership applies, as well, to changes in the group's task, or its technology, or any of many features of its embedding context. Many groups have frequent changes in their tasks. Other groups are responsible for a wide variety of tasks over time, with the current array of task activities at any given time reflecting organizational demands at that time. Any feature of group process and outcome that is sensitive to variations in tasks is vulnerable to changes in tasks over time. Similarly, the technology used by groups often is subject to change—especially when it is specific to tasks, and especially when it is new—and features of group process and outcome that are sensitive to variations in technology should be, on the face of it, vulnerable to changes in technology. Moreover, many groups inhabit contexts characterized by more or less frequent, more or less rapid, and more or less predictable changes relevant to the operation of those groups. Here, again, effects of technology (or any other input factors) on group process and performance are likely to interact with changes in features of the embedding context within which that group operates.

AN AGENDA FOR FUTURE RESEARCH ON TECHNOLOGY IN GROUPS

All of the issues discussed in this chapter suggest that the impact of technology in groups depends on a myriad of conditions and factors. How well a given group with a given technology fulfills its intended purposes depends not only on what function(s) the technological system is intended to serve (GCSS, GISS, GXSS, or GPSS) and on other features of that technology but also on attributes of the group and its members, on the type of task the group is doing, on the operating conditions under which they are working, and on the interaction of features of group, task, technology, and context. Furthermore, the impact of such technology on group process and performance operates in dynamic interdependence with key features of the group, task, and situation, and therefore is contingent on the detailed, specific history of the particular group, its task, and its circumstances. Group technology can have an impact on each of several key functions: internal and external communications, information access and processing, consensus generating and conflict resolution, and task performance. Technology can aid or hinder the group in its performance of processes that lie at the core of group existence: its development of norms, its member participation patterns, its members' satisfaction with themselves, their group, and its work. The technology can become an integral part of the meaning of the group as a continuing, dynamic, functional social system. Research should be carried out on those systems that is both more comprehensive and more systematic than what has been done so far, and that explores key issues within a long-term, context-embedded research paradigm.

There are a number of major themes and issues that we and other researchers in this field regard as crucial issues for future research on technology and groups, in order for that field to build such a cumulative knowledge base. Many of these themes and subthemes have been identified, more or less explicitly, in the research literature that we have reviewed on technology and groups; they are discussed in Chapters 2, 3, and 4 of this book. Most of them are echoed in the preceding sections of this chapter. Here, we will try to give voice to those themes and subthemes in a simplified but systematic manner.

The main message we convey here is that future research needs to be (a) more comprehensive with respect to the variables being studied; (b) more systematic with respect to the study of those variables, and their interactions, in ways that allow comparisons of findings across multiple studies; and (c) more concerned with studying long-term and in-context effects of the use of technology in groups, rather than with studying only short-run effects under context-stripped, relatively artificial operating conditions.

Figure 5.3 lists five major themes and a number of subthemes that we regard as some of the key issues that need to be addressed in future theoretical and empirical research on technology in groups. Those themes and subthemes constitute an agenda for strategically crucial research in this domain. We have already discussed most of the issues earlier; here, we will simply summarize them.

I. Multiple Criteria for Assessment

Task performance measures
Interaction process measures
User reactions

II. Variations in Member and Group Characteristics

Member attributes
Group composition and structure
Member-Group-Task-Technology interactions

III. Variations in Task and Technology Factors

Task types and characteristics
Technological systems
Task-Technology interactions

IV. Groups as Multifunction Systems

Information-processing systems
Consensus-generating, conflict-managing systems
Systems for motivating and regulating behavior

V. Impact of Changes Over Time

Group development changes
Changes regarding learning and task experience
Changes regarding group membership, task, technology, situation

Figure 5.3. Some Themes for Future Research

Theme I: *Use Multiple Criteria to Assess the Impact of Technology on Groups*

Use multiple criteria of group task performance (e.g., quality, quantity, cost) and interrelate them to one another.

Use multiple measures of user reactions for each of various stakeholders (e.g., indices of satisfaction with system by members, groups, and supporters in embedding context; indices of group and interpersonal satisfaction).

Use multiple indices of group interaction and performance processes that adequately reflect patterns of participation, indications of informational and normative influence, information-processing activities, indicators of consensus-building and conflict resolution activities, evidences of interpersonal and group relationships, and the like.

Develop a criterion system or theory of group performance that interrelates all of those sets of indices.

Theme II: Study Effects of Variations in Member and Group
Characteristics

Systematically vary a wide range of member attributes (e.g., abilities, experience, and attitudes regarding task and media).

Systematically vary a wide range of group attributes (e.g., size, formality, past history, and homogeneity or heterogeneity of members regarding a number of attributes).

Study how member and group attributes interact with task and technology factors (e.g., group and member experience with and attitudes regarding task, media).

Theme III: Study Effects of Variations in Task and Technology Factors

Study a wide range of variations in task types (e.g., idea generation, planning, problem solving, decision making, conflict resolving) that subsume all of the forms of tasks that most groups do.

Study variations in technological systems (e.g., GCSS vs. GISS vs. GPSS; spatial dispersion; synchronous vs. asynchronous).

Study interactions of task and technology (e.g., task-technology fit regarding information richness).

Theme IV: Study Groups as Multifunction Systems

Study how technology effects the operation of groups as information-processing systems (e.g., effects of technology on information-processing patterns, information distribution, and information sharing).

Study how technology effects groups as consensus-generating systems (e.g., effects of technology on speed and difficulty of development of consensus, and on the occurrence, recognition, resolution of intragroup conflict).

Study how technology effects the operation of groups as systems for motivating and regulating behavior in organizational settings (e.g., effects of electronic communication systems such as e-mail on extratask communication patterns, on satisfaction with job and organization, on ability to organize and/or acquire knowledge and expertise needed for tasks from outside own work group, and on patterns of interpersonal relationships, loyalties, and intangible rewards).

Theme V: *Study How Change Alters the Effects of Technology in Groups*

- Study group development as a change process altering the usefulness of technology (e.g., modifications in the impact of technology on groups arising from changes related to group developmental patterns, problem phase sequences, etc.).
- Study how technology is altered by group and organizational learning (e.g., modifications in impact of technology on groups arising from the embedding of the effects of prior experience in member skills and knowledge, in group structures and norms, and in technology and task procedures).
- Study how changes in the group's organizational and environmental context affect the uses and impact of technology (e.g., modifications in impact of technology on groups that arise from changes in group membership, tasks, technology, and operating conditions).

Some Normative Suggestions for the Research Community

As noted in Chapter 4, it is not possible to make strong comparisons of findings from past empirical studies in this domain because different researchers have studied different systems using different kinds of groups doing different kinds of tasks under varied conditions, and those studies have used different sets of outcome criteria as their dependent variables. When past research about technology and groups is aggregated, therefore, it does not constitute a tightly woven, cumulative body of information, but rather a scattered picture of noncomparable findings about relations between different independent and different dependent variables, for systems varying in group and member characteristics, tasks and task characteristics, technology and situational conditions. It is vital for any field to be able to cumulate its theoretical and empirical information, hence to be able to compile a knowledge base about which it can be confident.

In Chapter 4, we also pointed out a number of important difficulties that make the body of work in this area less cumulative than is desirable, and therefore make each piece of empirical research in this area less valuable than it could be—no matter how sound and imaginative that research study might be in and of itself. In that same vein, the research agenda outlined here emphasizes the need to broaden the range of both independent, dependent, and intervening or process variables to include in research.

It may seem to the reader that we are calling for every piece of research in this area to be so comprehensive in scope that it will be impossible to carry out in practice (if not indeed impossible in principle). It is our intention to encourage more research in this area, not to present a prescription that discourages active research interest in this domain.

Let us repeat a caveat from an earlier chapter: The implied criticisms about comprehensive and systematic research are not criticisms of individual studies. Indeed, no individual study can be comprehensive and systemic; that requires cumulation over studies. Our comments referred to the consequences for the field of study that arise from the (very desirable) free enterprise philosophy of research in the social and behavioral sciences. A series of studies by different researchers, each of which was reasonable and even quite compelling from the perspective of the individual researcher, can turn out, in the aggregate, to be far less compelling as a cumulative body of relevant information. There is no invisible hand underlying research that somehow makes collective work do "the greatest good. . . ." If anything, the invisible hand (or system forces) underlying the domain drive the collective body of information toward diverse, isolated, nonoverlapping sets of findings unconnected to an overall schema.

For a field to build a cumulative body of knowledge successfully, it must somehow overcome those dissipative system forces. This is difficult to do. There is a direct way to do this: by the establishment of some kind of overriding research directorate that controls and directs the research in this area. We reject that direct route categorically. That "cure" would be worse than the problem! But there are a number of partial, indirect, and subtle means by which a scientific community can bring about such an integrated body of work. We will try to identify some of these as potential steps for the community of scientists who will continue the study of technology in groups.

To help toward this aim, we here present a number of suggestions about how the community of scholars in this domain (or in any other domain of behavioral and social science knowledge) might try to reshape some of the institutional resources of the field so that the individual studies done in it can accumulate knowledge more effectively. These are not an exhaustive list; nor are they especially innovative or radical. Many are now done in this (and other) areas of study, at least to a limited degree. We urge more frequent use of these procedures, and invention of additional ones, to help make our common endeavor more integrative.

1. Plan studies from a comprehensive framework: Encourage all researchers to formulate their research problems systematically, within a broad, comprehensive context or conceptual framework—to acknowledge that many variables and criteria are potentially relevant and valuable—even though, in any one study, they will be able to manipulate, control, or measure only a few of them.
2. Reward integrative work: Develop norms that value (and reward) the development and presentation of both quantitative and qualitative meta-analyses of empirical evidence in defined portions of the field, and the development and presentation of integrative theoretical formulations.
3. Increase communication across laboratories: Establish venues in which researchers from different laboratories can communicate about current and impending research in some detail.
4. Crossbreed concepts and measures across laboratories: Develop norms that value (and reward) explicit cross-fertilization between laboratories by use of concepts and measures in the studies of a given laboratory that are central to the work done in other laboratories.
5. Crossbreed researchers across laboratories: Develop practices that encourage (and reward) collaborative research by scholars who work from different perspectives and who carry different viewpoints into those projects. In doing so, encourage cross-fertilization of personnel by development of postdoctoral exchange programs for temporary interchanges of scientific/professional personnel.

There is some evidence that a fairly high level of both colonization and cross-fertilization is already taking place with respect to key research personnel, key study concepts, and research facilities. For example: The University of Georgia has key faculty members trained in the University of Minnesota SAMM system (Rick Watson), others trained with the University of Arizona GroupSystems (Alan Dennis), and still others (Bob Bostrom) who combine training at Minnesota with research experience at the University of Indiana (which is itself to some degree an Arizona "colony"). Similarly, the University of Arizona has faculty with experience in the Rand/Claremont group (Barbara Gutek) and the Carnegie Mellon group (Suzanne Weisband). Regarding cross-testing of key study concepts: There is at least one study done jointly by the Hiltz and Minnesota groups; there is a pair of relatively parallel dissertations done at Minnesota (V. Sambamurthy) and Arizona (Annette Easton). All of these indications are favorable signs, not only of the vitality and ferment of the field, but also of active steps that will help alleviate some of the domain-level issues discussed earlier in this chapter.

CONCLUDING COMMENTS

Someone once said that war is too important to be left to the generals. To paraphrase, it might be argued that advanced technology in collaborative work may be too important to leave to the technologists. In our opinion, much more research is needed on what happens when advanced technology designed to help groups do their work is actually put to use by work groups in their day-to-day activities. We have had very rapid developments on the technological system side, and an outpouring of thoughtful and insightful conceptualizations of these matters, but empirical research to assess the usefulness of such technology has not kept pace. Above all, in our view, too little of that research has been concerned with group, theoretical, and temporal issues; and too little of it has been done in ways that cut across specific systems, topics, types of groups, and methodological issues.

These needs pose a dilemma for researchers in this field: More systematic and programmatic strategies are needed for the research domain as a whole; this implies some level of coordination among the various research groups working in this substantive area. Yet the very vitality and creativity of this (and most other) behavioral science research area is in large part driven by the opportunities each investigator has for innovative, independent lines of research. We hope that the material laid out in this book, and the research agenda presented in this chapter, can provide useful information and some direction for future research that will advance understanding of how groups interact with computers and other electronic technology.

Bibliography

This bibliography is more extensive than the usual list of references to literature cited in a book. It includes all of the publications that were cited as part of our review of empirical studies reported in Chapter 4 (for which annotations are presented in the appendix), as well as all of those cited in our review of theoretical literature in Chapter 3 and citations elsewhere in the book. In addition, the bibliography includes a large number of references to chapters, articles, and books that are an important part of the research and scholarly literature of this domain and that contributed to our literature review and integration, but that were not specifically cited in the text.

Abel, M. J. (1990). Experiences in an exploratory distributed organization. In J. Galegher, R. Kraut, & C. Egido (Eds.), *Intellectual teamwork: The sociological and technical bases of collaborative work* (pp. 489-510). Hillsdale, NJ: Lawrence Erlbaum.

Abel, M. J., Corey, D., Bulick, S., Schmidt, J., & Coffin, S. (1992). The US West advanced technologies telecollaboration research project. In G. Wagner (Ed.), *Computer augmented teamwork*. New York: Van Nostrand Reinhold.

Adelman, L. (1984). Real time computer support for decision analysis in a group setting: Another class of decision support systems. *Interfaces, 14,* 75-83.

Adrianson, L., & Hjelmquist, E. (1991). Group processes in face-to-face and computer-mediated communication. *Behaviour and Information Technology, 10*(4), 281-296.

Aldag, R. J., & Power, D. J. (1986). An empirical analysis of computer-aided decision analysis. *Decision Sciences, 17*(3), 572-587.

Allen, T. J., & Hauptman, O. (1987). The influence of communication technologies on organizational structure: A conceptual model for future research. *Communication Research, 14,* 575-587.

Ancona, D. G. (1987). Groups in organizations: Extending laboratory models. In C. Hendrick (Ed.), *Group processes and intergroup relations* (pp. 207-230). Newbury Park, CA: Sage.

Ancona, D. G. (1990a). Outward Bound: Strategies for team survival in the organization. *Academy of Management Journal, 33*(2), 334-365.

Ancona, D. G. (1990b). Top management teams: Preparing for the revolution. In J. Carroll (Ed.), *Applied social psychology and organizational settings* (pp. 99-128). Hillsdale, NJ: Lawrence Erlbaum.

Ancona, D. G., & Caldwell, D. E. (1987). Management issues facing new-product teams in high-technology companies. *Advances in Industrial and Labor Relations, 4*, 199-221.

Ancona, D. G., & Caldwell, D. E. (1988). Beyond task and maintenance: Defining external functions in groups. *Group & Organization Studies, 13*(4), 468-494.

Ancona, D. G., & Caldwell, D. E. (1989). *Demography and design: Predictors of new product team performance* (Working Paper No. 3078-89). Cambridge: Massachusetts Institute of Technology, Alfred P. Sloan School of Management.

Ancona, D. G., & Caldwell, D. E. (1990). Information technology and work groups: The case of new product teams. In J. Galegher, R. Kraut, & C. Egido (Eds.), *Intellectual teamwork: Social and technological foundations of cooperative work* (pp. 173-190). Hillsdale, NJ: Lawrence Erlbaum.

Argote, L., & McGrath, J. E. (1993). Group processes in organizations: Continuity and change. In C. L. Cooper & I. T. Robertson (Eds.), *International review of industrial and organizational psychology* (Vol. 8, pp. 333-389). Chichester, UK: Wiley.

Argyle, M., & Dean, J. (1965). Eye contact, distance, and affiliation. *Sociometry, 28*, 289-304.

Argyle, M., & Kendon, A. (1967). The experimental analysis of social performance. In L. Berkowitz (Ed.), *Advances in experimental social psychology* (Vol. 3, pp. 55-99). New York: Academic Press.

Arunachalam, V. (in press). Computer-mediated communication and structured interaction in transfer pricing negotiation. *Journal of Information Systems*.

Baecker, R. M. (Ed.). (1993). *Readings in groupware and computer-supported cooperative work: Assisting human-human collaboration*. San Mateo, CA: Morgan Kaufmann.

Barefoot, J., & Strickland, L. (1982). Conflict and dominance in television-mediated interactions. *Human Relations, 35*(7), 559-566.

Barfield, W., & Robless, R. (1989). The effects of two- or three-dimensional graphics on the problem-solving performance of experienced and novice decision makers. *Behaviour and Information Technology, 8*, 369-385.

Barley, S. (1988). On technology, time, and social order: Technically induced change in the temporal organization of radiological work. In F. Dubinskas (Ed.), *Making time ethnographies of high technology organizations* (pp. 123-169). Philadelphia: Temple University Press.

Beswick, R., & Reinsch, N., Jr. (1987). Attitudinal responses to voice mail. *Journal of Business Communication, 24*(3), 23-25.

Bikson, T. K., & Eveland, J. D. (1986). *New office technology: Planning for people* (Work in America Insititute's Series in Productivity). New York: Pergamon.

Bikson, T. K., & Eveland, J. D. (1990a). The interplay of work group structures and computer support. In J. Galegher, R. Kraut, & C. Egido (Eds.), *Intellectual teamwork: Social and technological foundations of cooperative work* (pp. 245-290). Hillsdale, NJ: Lawrence Erlbaum.

Bikson, T. K., & Eveland, J. D. (1990b). *Technology transfer as a framework for understanding social impacts of computerization* (Rand Note No. N-3113-NSF). Santa Monica, CA: RAND.

Bikson, T. K., Eveland, J. D., & Gutek, B. A. (1989). Flexible interactive technologies for multi-person tasks: Current problems and future prospects. In M. Olson (Ed.), *Technological support for work group collaboration* (pp. 89-112). Hillsdale, NJ: Lawrence Erlbaum.

Bikson, T. K., & Gutek, B. A. (1983). *Advanced office systems: An empirical look at use and satisfaction.* Santa Monica, CA: RAND.

Bikson, T. K., Gutek, B. A., & Mankin, D. A. (1987). *Implementing computerized procedures in office settings: Influences and outcomes* (Rand Publication Series paper ISI-8110792). Santa Monica, CA: RAND.

Bikson, T. K., & Schieber, L. (1990). *Relationships between electronic information media and records management practices: Results of a survey of United Nations organizations* (Rand Note No. N-3150-RC). Santa Monica, CA: RAND.

Blackwell, M. (1987). Electronic observations of computer user behavior. In S. Kiesler & L. Sproull (Eds.), *Computing and change on campus.* New York: Cambridge University Press.

Bui, T., Sivansankaran, T., Fijol, Y., & Woodburg, M. (1987). *Identifying organizational opportunities for GDSS use: Some experimental evidence.* Transactions of Seventh Conference on Decision Support Systems (pp. 68-75), San Francisco.

Burn, J. M. (1989). The impact of information technology on organizational structures. *Information and Management, 16,* 1-10.

Carley, K. (1984). *Electronic mail as a managerial tool* (Research paper RP 21). Carnegie Mellon University, Committee on Social Science Research in Computing, Pittsburgh, PA.

Chaiken, S., & Eagly, A. H. (1983). Communication modality as a determinant of persuasion: The role of communicator salience. *Journal of Personality and Social Psychology, 45,* 241-256.

Champness, B. G., & Reid, A.A.L. (1970). *The efficiency of information transmission: A preliminary comparison between face-to-face meetings and the telephone* (Tech. report No. P/70240/CH). Cambridge, UK: Post Office, Long Range Intelligence.

Chapanis, A., Ochsman, R. B., Parrish, R. N., & Weeks, G. D. (1972). Studies in interactive communication: The effects of four communication modes on behavior of teams during cooperative problem solving. *Human Factors, 14,* 487-509.

Chapanis, A., Ochsman, R. B., Parrish, R. N., & Weeks, G. D. (1977). Studies in interactive communication II: The effects of four communication modes on the linguistic performance of teams during cooperative problem solving. *Human Factors, 19,* 101-126.

Chapanis, A., & Overbey, C. M. (1974). Studies in interactive communication III: Effects of similar and dissimilar communication channels and two interchange options on team problem solving. *Perceptual and Motor Skills, 38,* 343-374.

Chidambaram, L., Bostrom, R. P., & Wynne, B. E. (1991). The impact of GDSS on group development. *Journal of Management Information Systems, 7*(3), 3-25.

Cicourel, A. (1990). The integration of distributed knowledge in collaborative medical diagnosis. In J. Galegher, R. Kraut, & C. Egido (Eds.), *Intellectual teamwork: Social and technological foundations of cooperative work* (pp. 221-242). Hillsdale, NJ: Lawrence Erlbaum.

Connolly, T., Jessup, L. M., & Valacich, J. S. (1989). Effects of anonymity and evaluative tone on idea generation in computer-mediated groups. *Management Science, 36,* 689-703.

Contractor, N., & Eisenberg, E. (1990). Communication networks and new media in organizations. In J. Fulk & C. Steinfield (Eds.), *Organizations and communication technology* (pp. 143-172). Newbury Park, CA: Sage.

Contractor, N., & Seibold, D. (1993). Theoretical frameworks for the study of structuring processes in group decision support systems: Adaptive structuration theory and self organizing systems theory. *Human Communication Research, 19*, 528-563.

Cooper, W. H., Gallupe, R. B., Bastianutti, L. M. (1990). Electronic vs. non-electronic brainstorming. *Proceedings of the Academy of Management*, 237-241.

Culnan, M. J., & Markus, M. L. (1987). Information technologies. In F. M. Jablin, L. L. Putnam, K. H. Roberts, & L. W. Porter (Eds.), *Handbook of organizational communication: An interdisciplinary perspective* (pp. 420-443). Newbury Park, CA: Sage.

Daft, R. L., & Lengel, R. H. (1984). Information richness: A new approach to managerial behavior and organizational design. *Research in Organizational Behavior, 6*, 191-233.

Daft, R. L., & Lengel, R. H. (1986). Organizational information requirements, media richness and structural design. *Management Science, 32*, 554-571.

Daft, R. L., Lengel, R. H., & Trevino, L. K. (1987). Message equivocality, media selection, and manager performance: Implication for information systems. *MIS Quarterly, 11*, 354-366.

Daft, R., & Weick, C. (1984). Toward a model of organizations as interpretation systems. *Academy of Management Review, 9*, 284-295.

Dalkey, N. C. (1969). The delphi method: An experimental study of group opinion. Santa Monica, CA: RAND.

Daly, B. (1993). The influence of face-to-face versus computer-mediated communication channels on collective induction. *Accounting, Management, & Information Technology, 3*(1), 1-22.

Dennis, A. R., & Gallupe, R. B. (1993). A history of group support systems empirical reserach: Lessons learned and future directions. In L. M. Jessup & J. S. Valacich (Eds.), *Group support sytems: New perspectives* (pp. 59-77). New York: Macmillan.

Dennis, A. R., George, J. F., Jessup, L. M., Nunamaker, J. F., & Vogel, D. R. (1988). Information technology to support electronic meetings. *MIS Quarterly, 12*, 591-624.

Dennis, A. R., Heminger, A., Nunamaker, J., & Vogel, D. (1990). Bringing automated support to large groups: The Burr-Brown experience. *Information and Management, 18*(3), 111-121.

Dennis, A. R., Nunamaker, J. F., & Vogel, D. (1991). A comparison of laboratory and field research in the study of electronic meeting systems. *Journal of Management Information Systems, 7*(3), 107-135.

Dennis, A. R., Valacich, J. S., & Nunamaker, J. (1990). An experimental investigation of the effects of group size in an electronic meeting environment. *IEEE Transactions on Systems, Man, & Cybernetics, 25*, 1049-1057.

DeSanctis, G., Dickson, G. W., Jackson, B. M., & Poole, M. S. (1991, August). *Using computing in the face-to-face meeting: Some initial observations from the Texaco-Minnesota project*. Paper presented at the 51st meeting of the Academy of Management, Miami, FL.

DeSanctis, G., D'Onofrio, M., Sambamurthy, V., & Poole, M. S. (1989). Comprehensiveness and restrictiveness in group decision heuristics: Effects of computer support on consensus decision making. In J. DeGross, J. Henderson, & B. Konsynski (Eds.), *Proceedings of the 10th International Conference on Information Systems* (pp. 131-140). Boston, MA: Society for Information Management.

DeSanctis, G., & Gallupe, R. B. (1987). A foundation for the study of group decision support systems. *Management Science, 33*(5), 589-609.

DeSanctis, G., & Gallupe, B. (1989). Group decision support systems: A new frontier. In R. Sprague & H. Watson (Eds.), *Decision support systems: Putting theory into practice* (2nd ed.). Englewood Cliffs, NJ: Prentice-Hall.

DeSanctis, G., & Poole, M. S. (1990). Understanding the differences in collaborative system use through appropriation analysis. In J. F. Nunamaker, Jr. (Ed.), *Proceedings of the 24th annual Hawaii International Conference on System Sciences* (Vol. 3, pp. 750-757). Los Alamitos, CA: IEEE Computer Society Press.

DeSanctis, G., Poole, M. S., Dickson, G. W., & Jackson, B. M. (in press). An interpretive analysis of team use of group technologies. *Journal of Organizational Computing.*

DeSanctis, G., Poole, M. S., Lewis, H., & Desharnais, G. (1991). Using computing in quality team meetings: Initial observations from the IRS-Minnesota Project. *Journal of Management Information Systems, 8*(3), 7-26.

Dickson, G., Lee, J., Robinson, L., & Heath, R. (1989). Observations on GDSS interaction: Chauffeured, facilitated, and user-driven systems. In R. Blanning & D. King (Eds.), *Proceedings of the 22nd annual Hawaii International Conference on System Sciences* (Vol. 3, pp. 337-343). Los Alamitos, CA: IEEE Computer Society Press.

Diehl, M., & Stroebe, W. (1987). Productivity loss in brainstorming groups: Toward the solution of a riddle. *Journal of Personality and Social Psychology, 53*(3), 497-509.

Diehl, M., & Stroebe, W. (1991). Productivity loss in brainstorming groups: Tracking down the blocking effect. *Journal of Personality and Social Psychology, 61,* 392-403.

Dubrovsky, V. J., Kiesler, S., & Sethna, B. N. (1991). The equalization phenomenon: Status effects in computer-mediated and face-to-face decision making groups. *Human-Computer Interaction, 6,* 119-146.

Duncanson, J. P., & Williams, A. D. (1973). Video conferencing: Reactions of users. *Human Factors, 15,* 471-485.

Dutton, J. E. (1988). Review of new technology as organizational innovation: The development and diffusion of microelectronics. *Academy of Management Review, 13*(3), 497-500.

Dutton, W. H., Fulk, J., & Steinfield, C. (1982). Utilization of video conferencing. *Telecommunications Policy, 6,* 164-178.

Easton, G., George, J., Nunamaker, J., & Pendergast, M. (1990). Using two different electronic meeting system tools for the same task: An experimental comparison. *Journal of Management Information Systems, 7*(1), 85-100.

Egido, C. (1990). Teleconferencing as a technology to support cooperative work: Its possibilities and limitations. In J. Galegher, R. Kraut, & C. Egido (Eds.), *Intellectual teamwork: Social and technological foundations of cooperative work* (pp. 351-372). Hillsdale, NJ: Lawrence Erlbaum.

Eils, L. C., & John, R. S. (1980). A criterion validation of multiattribute utility analysis and of group communication strategy. *Organizational Behavior & Human Performance, 25,* 268-288.

Ellis, C. A., Gibbs, S. J., & Rein, G. L. (1991). Groupware: Some issues and experiences. *Communications of the ACM, 34,* 39-58.

Elwork, A., & Gutkin, T. B. (1985). The behavioral sciences in the computer age. *Computers in Human Behavior, 1,* 3-18.

Eveland, J. D., & Bikson, T. K. (1989). Work group structures and computer support: A field experiment. *ACM Transactions on Office Information Systems, 6,* 354-379.

Finholt, T., & Sproull, L. (1990). Electronic groups at work. *Organizational Science, 1*(1), 41-64.

Finholt, T., Sproull, L., & Kiesler, S. (1990). Communication and performance in ad hoc groups. In J. Galegher, R. Kraut, & C. Egido (Eds.), *Intellectual teamwork: Social and technological foundations of cooperative work* (pp. 291-326). Hillsdale, NJ: Lawrence Erlbaum.

Fish, R. S., Kraut, R. E., & Root, R. W. (1993). Video as a technology for informal communication. *Communications of the ACM, 36,* 48-61.

Fleischer, M., & Morell, J. A. (1985). The organizational and managerial consequences of computer technology. *Computers in Human Behavior, 1,* 83-93.

Flynn, B. B., & Jacobs, F. R. (1987). An experimental comparison of cellular (group technology) layout with process layout. *Decision Sciences, 18*(4), 562-581.

Franz, C. R., & Robey, D. (1986). Organizational context, user involvement, and the usefulness of information systems. *Decision Sciences, 17*(3), 329-356.

Fulk, J., & Dutton, W. H. (1984). Videoconferencing as an organizational information system: Assessing the role of electronic meetings. *Systems, Objectives and Solutions, 4*(2), 105-118.

Fulk, J., Schmitz, J. W., & Steinfield, C. W. (1990). A social influence model of technology use. In J. Fulk & C. Steinfield (Eds.), *Organizations and communication technology* (pp. 117-140). Newbury Park, CA: Sage.

Fulk, J., Steinfield, C. W., Schmitz, J., & Power, J. G. (1987). A social information processing model of media use in organizations. *Communication Research, 14,* 529-552.

Gabarro, J. (1990). The development of working relationships. In J. Galegher, R. Kraut, & C. Egido (Eds.), *Intellectual teamwork: Social and technological foundations of cooperative work* (pp. 79-110). Hillsdale, NJ: Lawrence Erlbaum.

Galegher, J. (1990). Intellectual teamwork and information technology: The role of information systems in collaborative intellectual work. In J. S. Carroll (Ed.), *Applied social psychology and organizational settings* (pp. 193-216). Hillsdale, NJ: Lawrence Erlbaum.

Galegher, J., & Kraut, R. E. (1990). Technology for intellectual teamwork: Perspectives on research and design. In J. Galegher, R. Kraut, & C. Egido (Eds.), *Intellectual teamwork: The social and technological bases of cooperative work* (pp. 1-20). Hillsdale, NJ: Lawrence Erlbaum.

Galegher, J., Kraut, R. E., & Egido, C. (Eds.). (1990). *Intellectual teamwork: The social and technical bases of cooperative work.* Hillsdale, NJ: Lawrence Erlbaum.

Gallupe, R. B., Bastianutti, L. M., & Cooper, W. H. (1991). Unblocking brainstorms. *Journal of Applied Psychology, 76*(1), 137-142.

Gallupe, R. B., Dennis, A. R., Cooper, W. H., Valacich, J. S., Bastianutti, L. M., & Nunamaker, J. F. (1992). Electronic brainstorming and group size. *Academy of Management Journal, 35,* 350-369.

Gallupe, R. B., DeSanctis, G., & Dickson, G. (1988). Computer-based support for group problem solving: An experimental investigation. *MIS Quarterly, 12,* 277-296.

132   GROUPS INTERACTING WITH TECHNOLOGY

Gallupe, R. B., & McKeen, J. (1990). Enhancing computer-mediated communication: An experimental study into the use of a decision support system for face-to-face versus remote meetings. *Information and Management, 18,* 1-13.

Gattiker, U. E., Gutek, B. A., & Berger, D. E. (1988). Office technology and employee attitudes. *Social Science Computer Reviews, 6*(3), 327-340.

George, J., Easton, G., Nunamaker, J., & Northcraft, G. (1990). A study of collaborative group work with and without computer-based support. *Information Systems Research, 1*(4), 394-415.

Gersick, C. (1988). Time and transition in work teams: Toward a new model of group development. *Academy of Management Journal, 31*(1), 9-41.

Gersick, C. (1989). Marking time: Predictable transitions in task groups. *Academy of Management Journal, 32*(2), 274-309.

Goodman, G., & Abel, M. (1987). Communication and collaboration: Facilitating cooperative work through communication. *Office, Technology, and People, 3,* 129-146.

Goodman, P. G., & Sproull, L. S. (Eds.). (1990). *Technology and organizations.* San Francisco: Jossey-Bass.

Goslar, M. D., Green, G. I., & Hughes, T. H. (1986). Decision support systems: An empirical assessment for decision making. *Decision Sciences, 17*(1), 79-91.

Gray, P., & Nunamaker, J. (1989). Group decision support systems. In R. Sprague & R. Watson (Eds.), *Decision support systems: Putting theory into practice* (chap. 19). Englewood Cliffs, NJ: Prentice-Hall.

Greenberg, S. (Ed.). (1991). *Computer supported cooperative work and group ware.* New York: Praeger.

Grief, I. (Ed.). (1988). *Computer-supported cooperative work: A book of readings.* San Mateo, CA: Morgan Kaufmann.

Gruenfeld, D. H., & Hollingshead, A. B. (1993). Sociocognition in work groups: The evolution of group integrative complexity and its relation to task performance. *Small Group Research, 24*(3), 383-405.

Gutek, B. A. (1990). Work group structure and information technology: A structural contingency approach. In J. Galegher, R. Kraut, & C. Egido (Eds.), *Intellectual teamwork: The social and technical bases of cooperative work* (pp. 63-78). Hillsdale, NJ: Lawrence Erlbaum.

Gutek, B. A., & Bikson, T. K. (1985). Differential experiences of men and women in computerized offices. *Sex Roles, 13,* 123-136.

Gutek, B. A., Bikson, T. K., & Mankin, D. (1985). Individual and organizational consequences of computer-based office information technology. In S. Oskamp (Ed.), *Applied social psychology annual: Vol. 5. Applications in organizational settings* (pp. 231-254). Beverly Hills, CA: Sage.

Gutek, B. A., & Winter, S. J. (1990). Computer use, control over computers and job satisfaction. In S. Oskamp & S. Spacapan (Eds.), *People's reactions to technology in factories, offices, and aerospace* (pp. 121-144). Newbury Park, CA: Sage.

Haas, C. (1989). Does the medium make a difference? Two studies of writing with pen and paper and with computers. *Human-Computer Interaction, 4,* 149-169.

Hackman, J. R., & Morris, C. G. (1975). Group tasks, group interaction process, and group performance effectiveness: A review and proposed integration. In L. Berkowitz (Ed.), *Advances in experimental psychology* (pp. 45-99). New York: Academic Press.

Hahm, W., & Bikson, T. (1990). Retirees using e-mail and networked computers (Rand Note No. N-3114-MF). Santa Monica, CA: RAND.

Hartmann, H. I., Kraut, R. E., & Tilly, L. A. (Eds.). (1986). *Computer chips and paper clips: Technology and women's employment.* Washington, DC: National Academy Press.

Hesse, B. W., Werner, C. M., & Altman, I. (1990). Temporal aspects of computer-mediated communication. *Computers in Human Behavior, 4,* 147-165.

Hiltz, S. R. (1988). Productivity enhancement for computer-mediated communication: A system contingency approach. *Communications of the ACM, 31,* 1428-1454.

Hiltz, S. R., Dufner, D., Holmes, M., & Poole, M. S. (1991). Distributed group support systems: Social dynamics and design dilemmas. *Journal of Organizational Computing, 2*(1), 135-159.

Hiltz, S. R., & Johnson, K. (1990). User satisfaction with computer-mediated communication systems. *Management Science, 36,* 739-764.

Hiltz, S. R., Johnson, K., & Turoff, M. (1986). Experiments in group decision making, 1: Communication process and outcome in face-to-face versus computerized conferences. *Human Communication Research, 13*(2), 225-252.

Hiltz, S. R., Johnson, K., & Turoff, M. (1991). Group decision support: The effects of designated human leaders and statistical feedback in computerized conferences. *Journal of Management Information Systems, 8,* 81-108.

Hiltz, S. R., & Turoff, M. (1978). *The network nation: Human communication via computer.* Reading, MA: Addison-Wesley.

Hiltz, S. R., & Turoff, M. (1985). Structuring computer-mediated communication systems to avoid information overload. *Communications of the ACM, 28,* 680-689.

Hiltz, S. R., Turoff, M., & Johnson, K. (1988). Experiments in group decision making, 3: Disinhibition, deindividuation, and group process in pen name and real name computer conferences. *Decision Support Systems, 5,* 1-16.

Ho, T. H., & Raman, K. S. (1991). The effects of GDSS and elected leadership on small group meetings. *Journal of Management Information Systems, 8,* 109-134.

Hollingshead, A. B. (1993). *Information, influence and technology in group decision making.* Unpublished doctoral dissertation, University of Illinois, Urbana-Champaign.

Hollingshead, A. B., & McGrath, J. E. (in press). The whole is less than the sum of its parts: A critical review of research on computer-assisted groups. In R. A. Guzzo & E. Salas (Eds.), *Team decision and team performance in organizations.* San Francisco: Jossey-Bass.

Hollingshead, A. B., McGrath, J. E., & O'Connor, K. M. (1993). Group task performance and communication technology: A longitudinal study of computer-mediated versus face-to-face work groups. *Small Group Research, 24*(3), 307-333.

Huber, G. P. (1990). A theory of the effects of advanced information technologies on organizational design. *Academy of Management Review, 15,* 47-71.

Huber, G. P., Cummings, L. L., & Arendt, E. (1974). Effects of size and spatial arrangements on group decision-making. *Academy of Management Journal, 17,* 460-475.

Huber, G. P., Valacich, J. S., & Jessup, L. M. (1993). A theory of the effects of group support systems on an organization's nature and decisions. In L. M. Jessup & J. S. Valacich (Eds.), *Group support systems: New perspectives* (pp. 255-269). New York: Macmillan.

Huff, C., Sproull, L. S., & Kiesler, S. (1989). Computer communication and organizational commitment: Tracing the relationship in a city government. *Journal of Applied Social Psychology, 19,* 1371-1391.

Hutchins, E. (1990). Technology in the cooperative work of navigation. In J. Galegher, R. Kraut, & C. Egido (Eds.), *Intellectual teamwork: Social and technological foundations of cooperative work* (pp. 191-220). Hillsdale, NJ: Lawrence Erlbaum.

Igbaria, M., Pavri, F. N., & Huff, S. L. (1989). Microcomputer applications: An empirical look at usage. *Information and Management, 16,* 187-196.

Ives, B., Olson, M., & Baroudi, J. (1983). The measurement of user information satisfaction. *Communications of the ACM, 26,* 783-793.

Jarvenpaa, S. L., Rao, R. S., & Huber, G. P. (1988). Computer support for meetings of medium-sized groups working on unstructured problems: A field experiment. *MIS Quarterly, 12,* 645-665.

Jessup, L. M. (1987). Group decision support systems: A need for behavioral research. *International Journal of Small Group Research, 3,* 139-158.

Jessup, L. M., Connolly, T., & Galegher, J. (1990). The effects of anonymity on GDSS group process with an idea-generating task. *MIS Quarterly, 14,* 312-321.

Jessup, L. M., Connolly, T., & Tansik, D. (1990). Toward a theory of automated group work: The deindividuating effects of anonymity. *Small Group Research, 21,* 333-348.

Jessup, L. M., & Tansik, D. A. (1991). Group problem solving in an automated environment: The effects of anonymity and proximity on group process and outcome with a group decision support system. *Decision Sciences, 22*(2), 266-279.

Jessup, L. M., & Valacich, J. S. (Eds.). (1993). *Group support systems: New perspectives.* New York: Macmillan.

Johansen, R. (1977). Social evaluations of teleconferencing. *Telecommunications Policy, 1,* 395-491.

Johansen, R. (1989). *Groupware: Computer support for business teams.* New York: Free Press.

Johansen, R., Vallee, J., & Spangler, K. (1979). *Electronic meetings: Technical alternatives and social choices.* Menlo Park, CA: Addison-Wesley.

Katz, R., & Tushman, M. (1990). Communication patterns, project performance, and task characteristics: An empirical evaluation and integration in an R&D setting. *Organizational Behavior and Human Decision Processes, 23,* 139-162.

Kazanjian, R. K. (1988). Relation of dominant problems to stages of growth in technology-based new ventures. *Academy of Management Journal, 31*(2), 257-279.

Keen, P.G.W. (1987). Telecommunications and organizational choice. *Communication Research, 14,* 588-606.

Kelly, J. R., Futoran, G. C., & McGrath, J. E. (1990). Capacity and capability: Seven studies of entrainment of task performance rates. *Small Group Research, 21,* 283-314.

Kiesler, S. (1986). The hidden messages in computer networks. *Harvard Business Review, 64*(1), 46-59.

Kiesler, S., Siegel, J., & McGuire, T. W. (1984). Social psychological aspects of computer-mediated communication. *American Psychologist, 39,* 1123-1134.

Kiesler, S., & Sproull, L. S. (1986). Response effects in the electronic survey. *Public Opinion Quarterly, 50,* 402-413.

Kiesler, S., & Sproull, L. S. (Eds.). (1987). *Computing and change on campus.* New York: Cambridge University Press.

Kiesler, S., & Sproull, L. S. (1992). Group decision making and communication technology. *Organizational Behavior and Human Decision Processes, 52,* 96-123.

Kiesler, S., Sproull, L. S., & Eccles, J. (1985). Poolhalls, chips, and war games: Women in the culture of computing. *Psychology of Women Quarterly, 9*, 451-462.

Kiesler, S., Zubrow, D., Moses, A. M., & Geller, V. (1985). Affect in computer-mediated communication: An experiment in synchronous terminal-to-terminal discussion. *Human Computer Interaction, 1*, 77-104.

King, J. L., & Star, S. L. (1990). Conceptual foundations for the development of organizational decision support systems. In J. Nunamaker (Ed.), *Proceedings of the Hawaii International Conference on Systems Science* (Vol. 3, pp. 143-151). Washington, DC: IEEE Press.

King, W. R., & Premkumar, G. (1989). Key issues in telecommunications planning. *Information and Management, 17*, 255-265.

Korzenny, F., & Bower, C. (1981). Testing a theory of electronic propinquity: Organizational teleconferencing. *Communication Research, 8*(4), 479-498.

Kraemer, K. L., & King, J. L. (1988). Computer-based systems for cooperative work and group decision making. *ACM Computing Surveys, 20*(2), 115-146.

Kraemer, K. L., & Pinsonneault, A. (1990). Technology and groups: Assessments of the empirical research. In J. Galegher, R. Kraut, & C. Egido (Eds.), *Intellectual teamwork: Social and technological foundations of cooperative work* (pp. 373-404). Hillsdale, NJ: Lawrence Erlbaum.

Krauss, R. M., & Fussel, S. R. (1990). Mutual knowledge and communication effectiveness. In J. Galegher, R. Kraut, & C. Egido (Eds.), *Intellectual teamwork: Social and technological foundations of cooperative work* (pp. 111-146). Hillsdale, NJ: Lawrence Erlbaum.

Kraut, R., Dumais, S., & Koch, S. (1989). Computers' impact on productivity and quality of work-life. *Communications of the ACM, 32*, 220-238.

Kraut, R. E., Egido, C., & Galegher, J. (1990). Patterns of contact and communication in scientific research collaborations. In J. Galegher, R. E. Kraut, & C. Egido (Eds.), *Intellective teamwork: Social and intellectual foundations of cooperative work* (pp. 149-172). Hillsdale, NJ: Lawrence Erlbaum.

Kraut, R. E., Fish, R. S., Root, R. W., & Chalfonte, B. L. (1990). Informal communication in organizations: Form, function, and technology. In S. Oskamp & S. Spacapan (Eds.), *People's reactions to technology in factories, offices, and aerospace* (pp. 145-202). Newbury Park, CA: Sage.

Kraut, R., Galegher, J., Fish, R., & Chalfone, B. (1992). Task requirements and media choice in collaborative writing. *Human-Computer Interaction, 7*, 375-407.

Kriebel, C. H., & Strong, D. M. (1984). A survey of the MIS and telecommunications activities of major business firms. *MIS Quarterly, 8*, 171-177.

Lai, K., Malone, T. W., & Yu, K. (1988). Object lens: A "spreadsheet" for cooperative work. *ACM Transactions on Office Information Systems, 6*(4), 332-353.

Lakin, F. (1990). Visual languages for cooperation: A performing medium approach to systems for cooperative work. In J. Galegher, R. Kraut, & C. Egido (Eds.), *Intellectual teamwork: Social and technological foundations of cooperative work* (pp. 453-488). Hillsdale, NJ: Lawrence Erlbaum.

Lamm, H., & Trommsdorff, G. (1973). Group versus individual performance on tasks requiring ideational proficiency (brainstorming): A review. *European Journal of Social Psychology, 3*(4), 361-388.

Landow, G. P. (1990). Hypertext and collaborative work: The example of intermedia. In J. Galegher, R. Kraut, & C. Egido (Eds.), *Intellectual teamwork: Social and tech-

nological foundations of cooperative work (pp. 407-428). Hillsdale, NJ: Lawrence Erlbaum.

LaPlante, A. (1989a). IBM study: PC's aid in decision process. *Infoworld, 11*(49), 1-8.

LaPlante, A. (1989b). Workgroup idea still unclear to users. *Infoworld, 11*(50), 1, 5.

Lea, M. (Ed.). (in press). *The social contexts of computer-mediated communication*. Hemmel Hempstead, UK: Harvester-Wheatsheaf.

Lea, M., & Spears, R. (1991). Computer-mediated communication, de-individuation, and group decision making. *International Journal of Man-Machine Studies, 34*, 283-301.

Levine, J. M., & Moreland, R. L. (1991). Culture and socialization in work groups. In L. B. Resnick, J. M. Levine, & S. D. Teasley (Eds.), *Perspectives on socially shared cognition* (pp. 257-279). Washington, DC: American Psychological Association.

Levine, J. M., Resnick, L. B., & Higgins, T. (1993). Social foundations of cognition. *Annual Review of Psychology, 44*, 585-612.

Lewis, S. A., & Fry, W. R. (1977). Effects of visual access and orientation on the discovery of integrative bargaining alternatives. *Organizational Behavior and Human Performance, 20*, 75-92.

Losada, M., Sanchez, P., & Noble, E. E. (1990). Collaborative technology and group process feedback: Their impact on interactive sequence in meetings. In F. Halasz (Ed.), *CSCW 90: Proceedings of the Conference on Computer-Supported Cooperative Work* (pp. 53-64). Los Angeles, CA: Association for Computing Machinery.

Malone, T. W. (1988). Organizing information processing systems: Parallels between human organizations and computer systems. In W. Zachery, S. Robertson, & J. Black (Eds.), *Cognition, computation, and cooperation*. Norwood, NJ: Ablex.

Malone, T. W., & Crowston, T. W. (1990). What is coordination theory and how can it help design cooperative work systems? In F. Halasz (Ed.), *CSCW 90: Proceedings of the Conference on Computer-Supported Cooperative Work* (pp. 357-370). Los Angeles, CA: Association for Computing Machinery.

Malone, T. W., Grant, K. R., Turbak, F. A., Brobst, S. A., & Cohen, M. D. (1987). Intelligent information-sharing systems. *Communications of the ACM, 30*, 390-402.

Malone, T. W., Yates, J., & Benjamin, R. I. (1987). Electronic markets and electronic hierarchies. *Communications of the ACM, 30*, 484-497.

Mankin, D., Bikson, T. K., & Gutek, B. A. (1984). Factors in successful implementation of computer-based office information systems: A review of the literature with suggestions for OBM research. *Journal of Organizational Behavior Management, 6*, 1-20.

Mantei, M. (1989). Observation of executives using a computer supported meeting environment. *Decision Support Systems, 5*, 153-166.

Markus, M. L. (1987). Toward a critical mass theory of interactive media: Universal access, interdependence and diffusion. *Communication Research, 14*, 491-511.

Markus, M. L., & Robey, D. (1988). Information technology and organizational change: Causal structure in theory and research. *Management Science, 5*, 583-587.

McCartt, A. T., & Rohrbaugh, J. (1989). Evaluating group decision support system effectiveness: A performance study of decision conferencing. *Decision Support Systems, 5*, 243-254.

McGrath, J. E. (1984). *Groups: Interaction and performance*. Englewood Cliffs, NJ: Prentice-Hall.

McGrath, J. E. (1990). Time matters in groups. In J. Galegher, R. Kraut, & C. Egido (Eds.), *Intellectual teamwork: Social and technological foundations of cooperative work* (pp. 23-61). Hillsdale, NJ: Lawrence Erlbaum.

McGrath, J. E. (1991). Time, interaction, and performance (TIP): A theory of groups. *Small Group Research, 22*, 147-174.

McGrath, J. E. (1993). Introduction: The JEMCO Workshop: Description of a longitudinal study. *Small Group Research, 24*, 285-306.

McGrath, J. E., Arrow, H., Gruenfeld, D. H, Hollingshead, A. B., & O'Connor, K. M. (1993). Groups, tasks, and technology: The effects of experience and change. *Small Group Research, 24*, 406-420.

McGrath, J. E., & Gruenfeld, D. H. (1993). Toward a dynamic and systemic theory of groups: An integration of six temporally enriched perspectives. In M. Chemers & R. Ayman (Eds.), *Leadership theory and research: Perspectives and directions* (pp. 217-243). New York: Academic Press.

McGrath, J. E., & Hollingshead, A. B. (1993). Putting the "Group" back in group support systems: Some theoretical issues about dynamic processes in groups with technological enhancements. In L. M. Jessup & J. S. Valacich (Eds.), *Group support systems: New perspectives* (pp. 78-96). New York: Macmillan.

McGrath, J. E., & Kelly, J. R. (1986). *Time and human interaction: Toward a social psychology of time.* New York: Guilford.

McGrath, J. E., Martin, J., & Kulka, R. A. (1982). *Judgment calls in research.* Beverly Hills, CA: Sage.

McGuire, T. W., Kiesler, S., & Siegel, J. (1987). Group and computer-mediated discussion effects in risk decision making. *Journal of Personality and Social Psychology, 52*, 917-930.

McKenney, J. L. (1988). *How managerial use of electronic mail influences organizational information processing: An exploratory study* (Working Paper 88-067). Cambridge: Harvard Business School, Division of Research.

McKenney, J. L., Doherty, V. S., & Sciokla, J. J. (1989). *An appraisal of how task evolution influences choice and use of communication media in management* (Working Paper No. 89-039). Cambridge: Harvard Business School, Division of Research.

McLeod, P. L. (1991, August). *What if Jesus had communicated with his apostles with a computer? Collaborative technology use by some famous groups.* Paper presented at the Academy of Management annual meeting, Miami, FL.

McLeod, P. L. (1992). An assessment of the experimental literature on the electronic support of group work: Results of a meta-analysis. *Human Computer Interaction, 7*(3), 257-280.

McLeod, P. L., & Liker, J. K. (1992). Electronic meeting systems: Evidence from a low structure environment. *Information Systems Research, 3*(3), 195-223.

McLeod, P. L., Liker, J. K., & Lobel, S. A. (1992). Process feedback in task groups: An application of goal setting. *Journal of Applied Behavioral Science, 28*(1), 15-41.

Melone, N. P. (1990). A theoretical assessment of the user-satisfaction construct in information systems research. *Management Science, 36*(1), 76-91.

Mennecke, B. E., Hoffer, J. A., & Wynne, B. E. (1992). The implications of group development and history for group support system theory and practice. *Small Group Research, 23*, 524-572.

Minch, R. P., & Sanders, G. L. (1986). Computerized information systems supporting multicriteria decision making. *Decision Sciences, 17*(3), 395-413.

Moreland, R. L., & Levine, J. M. (1992). The composition of small groups. In E. L. Lawler, B. Markovsky, C. Ridgeway, & H. Walker (Eds.), *Advances in group processes* (Vol. 9, pp. 237-280). Greenwich, CT: JAI.

Morell, J. A. (1988, Fall/Winter). The organizational consequences of office automation: Refining measurement techniques. *Data Base*, pp. 16-23.

Myers, D. (1987). "Anonymity is part of the magic": Individual manipulation of computer-mediated communication contexts. *Qualitative Sociology, 10*, 251-266.

Nunamaker, J. F., Applegate, L., & Konsynski, B. (1988). Computer-aided deliberation: Model management and group decision support. *Journal of Operations Research, 3*, 5-19.

Nunamaker, J. F., Dennis, A. R., Valacich, J. S. (1991). Information technology for negotiating groups: Generating options for mutual gain. *Management Science, 37*, 1325-1346.

Nunamaker, J. F., Dennis, A. R., Valacich, J. S., Vogel, D. R., & George, J. F. (1991). Electronic meeting systems to support group work: Theory and practice at Arizona. *Communications of the ACM, 34*, 40-61.

Nunamaker, J. F., Vogel, D., Heminger, A., Martz, B., Grohowski, R., & McGoff, C. (1989). Experiences at IBM with group support systems: A field study. *Decision Support Systems: The International Journal, 5*(2), 183-196.

Nunamaker, J. F., Vogel, D., & Konsynski, B. (1989). Interaction of task and technology to support large groups. *Decision Support Systems: The International Journal, 5*(2), 139-152.

Olson, G. M., & Atkins, D. E. (1990). Supporting collaboration with advanced multimedia electronic mail: The NSF EXPRES project. In J. Galegher, R. Kraut, & C. Egido (Eds.), *Intellectual teamwork: Social and technological foundations of cooperative work* (pp. 429-452). Hillsdale, NJ: Lawrence Erlbaum.

Olson, G. M., & Olson, J. S. (1992). Defining a metaphor for group work. *IEEE Software, 9*(3), 93-95.

Olson, G. M., Olson, J. S., Carter, M., & Storrosten, M. (1992). Small group design meetings: An analysis of collaboration. *Human-Computer Interaction, 7*(4), 347-374.

Olson, G. M., Olson, J. R., McGuffin, L., Mack, L. A., Cornell, P., & Luchetti, R. (in press). Designing flexible space for the support of collaboration. In S. Kinney, R. Bostrom, & R. Watson (Eds.), *Computer augmented teamwork: A guided tour.* New York: Van Nostrand Reinhold.

Olson, G. M., Olson, J. S., Storrosten, M., Herbsleb, J., & Reuter, H. (in press). The structure of activity during design meetings. In T. Moran & J. Carroll (Eds.), *Design rationale.* Hillsdale, NJ: Lawrence Erlbaum.

Olson, J. S., Card, S. K., Landaurer, T. K., Olson, G. M., Malone, T., & Leggett, T. (1993). Computer supported cooperative work: Research issues for the 1990's. *Behaviour and Information Technology, 12*(2), 115-129.

Oren, T. I. (1984). Model-based information technology: Computer and system theoretic foundations. *Behavioral Sciences, 29*, 179-185.

Osborn, A. F. (1957). *Applied imagination* (2nd ed.). New York: Charles Scribner's Sons.

Pinsonneault, A., & Kraemer, K. L. (1989). The impact of technological support on groups: An assessment of the empirical research. *Decision Support Systems, 5*, 197-216.

Poole, M. S. (1983). Decision development in small groups, III: A multiple sequence model of group decision development. *Communication Monographs, 50,* 321-341.

Poole, M. S. (1991). Procedures for managing meetings: Social and technological innovation. In R. Swanson & B. Knapp (Eds.), *Innovative meeting management* (pp. 53-110). Austin, TX: 3M Meeting Management Institute.

Poole, M. S., & DeSanctis, G. (1989). Use of group decision support systems as an appropriation process. In *Proceedings of the 22nd annual Hawaii International Conference on System Sciences* (Vol. 4, pp. 149-157). Los Alamitos, CA: IEEE Computer Society Press.

Poole, M. S., & DeSanctis, G. (1990). Understanding the use of group decision support systems: The theory of adaptive structuration. In J. Fulk & C. Steinfield (Eds.), *Organizations and communication technology* (pp. 175-195). Newbury Park, CA: Sage.

Poole, M. S., & DeSanctis, G. (1992). Microlevel structuration in computer-supported group decision making. *Human Communication Research, 19*(1), 5-49.

Poole, M. S., Holmes, M., & DeSanctis, G. (1991). Conflict management in a computer-supported meeting environment. *Management Science, 37*(8), 926-953.

Poole, M. S., & Roth, J. (1988a). Decision development in small groups, IV: A typology of group decision paths. *Human Communication Research, 15*(3), 323-356.

Poole, M. S., & Roth, J. (1988b). Decision development in small groups, V: Test of a contingency model. *Human Communication Research, 15*(4), 549-589.

Putnam, L. L. (1979). Preference for procedural order in task oriented small groups. *Communication Monographs, 46,* 193-218.

Putnam, L. L. (1983). Small group work climates: A lag-sequential analysis of group interaction. *Small Group Behavior, 14*(4), 465-494.

Rapaport, M. (1991). *Computer-mediated communications: Bulletin boards, computer conferencing, electronic mail, information retrieval.* New York: Wiley.

Rawlins, C. (1989). The impact of teleconferencing on the leadership of small decision-making groups. *Journal of Organizational Behavior Management, 10*(2), 37-52.

Reder, S., & Schwab, R. (1989). The communicative economy of the workgroup: Multichannel genres of communication. *Office: Technology and People, 4*(3), 177-195.

Reid, A.A.L. (1971). *The telecommuniction impact model.* (Communication Studies Group Paper No. P/70244/RD). London: University College, School of Environmental Studies.

Rice, R. (1980a). Computer conferencing. In B. Dervin & M. Voigt (Eds.), *Progress in communication sciences* (Vol. 2). Norwood, NJ: Ablex.

Rice, R. (1980b). The impacts of computer-mediated organizational and interpersonnel communication. In M. Williams (Ed.), *Annual review of information science and technology* (Vol. 15, pp. 221-250). White Plains, NY: Knowledge Industry.

Rice, R. (1982). Communication networking in computer-conferencing systems: A longitudinal study of group roles and system structure. In M. Burgoon (Ed.), *Communication yearbook* (Vol. 6, pp. 925-944). Beverly Hills, CA: Sage.

Rice, R. E. (1984). *The new media: Communication, research and technology.* Beverly Hills, CA: Sage.

Rice, R. E. (1987). Computer-mediated communication and organizational innovation. *Journal of Communication, 37,* 65-94.

Rice, R. (1989). Computer-mediated communication system network data: Theoretical concerns and empirical examples. *International Journal Management-Machine Studies, 30*, 1-21.

Rice, R. (1990). From adversity to diversity: Applications of communication technology to crisis management. In T. Housel & J. Sleth (Eds.), *Information systems and crisis management*. New York: JAI.

Rice, R. E., & Case, D. (1983). Electronic message systems in the university: A description of use and utility. *Journal of Communication, 33*(1), 131-152.

Rice, R., & Contractor, N. S. (1990). Conceptualizing effects of office information systems: A methodology and application for the study of Alpha, Beta, and Gamma change. *Decision Sciences, 21*(2), 301-317.

Rice, R., Grant, A. E., Schmitz, J., & Totobin, J. (1990). Individual and network influences on the adoption and perceived outcomes of electronic messaging. *Social Networks, 12*(1), 27-55.

Rice, R., Hughes, D., & Love, G. (1989). Usage and outcomes of electronic messaging at an R&D organization: Situational constraints, job level, and media awareness. *Office: Technology and People, 5*(2), 141-161.

Rice, R. E., & Love, G. (1987). Electronic emotion: Socioemotional content in a computer-mediated network. *Communication Research, 14*, 85-108.

Rice, R., & Shook, D. E. (1988). Access to, usage of, and outcomes from an electronic messaging system. *ACM Transactions of Office Information Systems, 6*(3), 255-276.

Rice, R., & Shook, D. E. (1990a). Relationships of job categories and organizational levels to use of communication channels, including electronic mail: A meta-analysis and extension. *Journal of Management Studies, 27*, 195-229.

Rice, R., & Shook, D. E. (1990b). Voice messaging, coordination and communication. In J. Galegher, R. Kraut, & C. Egido (Eds.), *Intellectual teamwork: Social and technological foundations of cooperative work* (pp. 327-350). Hillsdale, NJ: Lawrence Erlbaum.

Rice, R., & Steinfield, C. (1991). New forms of organizational communication via electronic mail and voice messaging. In J. H. Andriessen & R. Roe (Eds.), *Telematics and work*. New York: Wiley.

Ruback, R. B., Dabbs, J. M., & Hopper C. H. (1984). The process of brainstorming: An analysis with individual and group vocal parameters. *Journal of Personality and Social Psychology, 47*, 558-567.

Rutter, D. R., & Robinson, B. (1980). An experimental analysis of teaching by telephone: Theoretical and practical implications for social psychology. In G. M. Stephenson & J. H. Davis (Eds.), *Progress in applied social psychology* (Vol. 1, pp. 345-374). London: Wiley.

Rutter, D. R., & Stephenson, G. M. (1975). The role of visual communication in synchronizing conversation. *European Journal of Social Psychology, 7*, 29-37.

Sabherwal, R., & Grover, V. (1989). Computer support for strategic decision-making processes: Review and analysis. *Decision Sciences, 20*(1), 54-76.

Sambamurthy, V., DeSanctis, G., & Poole, M. S. (in press). The effects of alternative computer-based designs on equivocality reduction during group decision-making. *Information Systems Research*.

Sambamurthy, V., & Poole, M. S. (in press). The effects of variations in capabilities of GDSS designs on management of cognitive conflict in groups. *Information Systems Research*.

Schmitz, J., & Fulk, J. (1991). Organizational colleagues, media richness, and electronic mail. *Communication Research, 18*(4), 487-523.

Short, J. A. (1974). Effects of medium of communication on experimental negotiation. *Human Relations, 27,* 225-234.

Short, J. A., Williams, E., & Christie, B. (1976). *The social psychology of telecommunications.* London: Wiley.

Shulman, A. D., Penman, R., & Sless, D. (1990). Putting information technology in its place: Organizational communication and the human infrastructure. In J. Carroll, *Applied social psychology and organizational settings* (pp. 155-192). Hillsdale, NJ: Lawrence Erlbaum.

Siegel, J., Dubrovsky, V., Kiesler, S., & McGuire, T. W. (1986). Group processes in computer-mediated communication. *Organizational Behavior & Human Decision Processes, 37,* 157-187.

Smith, J., & Vanecek, M. (1988). Computer conferencing and task-oriented decisions: Implications for group decision support. *Information and Management, 14,* 123-132.

Smith, J., & Vanecek, M. (1990). Dispersed group decision making using nonsimultaneous computer conferencing: A report of research. *Journal of Management Science, 7*(2), 71-92.

Spears, R., Lea, M., & Lee, S. (1990). De-individuation and group polarization in computer-mediated communication. *British Journal of Social Psychology, 29,* 121-134.

Sproull, L. S. (1986). Using electronic mail for data collection in organizational research. *Academy of Management Journal, 29,* 159-169.

Sproull, L. S., & Kiesler, S. (1986). Reducing social context cues: Electronic mail in organizational communication. *Management Science, 32*(11), 1492-1512.

Sproull, L. S., & Kiesler, S. (1991a). Computers, networks & work. *Scientific American, 265,* 116-123.

Sproull, L. S., & Kiesler, S. (1991b). *Connections: New ways of working in the networked organization.* Cambridge: MIT Press.

Sproull, L. S., Zubrow, D., & Kiesler, S. (1987). Cultural socialization to computing in college. *Computers in Human Behavior, 3,* 257-275.

Stasser, G., & Stewart, D. (1992). Discovery of hidden profiles by decision-making groups: Solving a problem versus making a judgment. *Journal of Personality and Social Psychology, 63,* 426-434.

Steeb, R., & Johnston, S. C. (1981). A computer-based interactive system for group decision-making. *IEEE Transactions on Systems, Man, and Cybernetics, SMC-11*(8), 544-552.

Stefik, M., Foster, G., Bobrow, D., Kahn, K., Lanning, S., & Suchman, L. (1987). Beyond the chalkboard: Computer support for collaboration and problem solving in meetings. *Communications of the ACM, 30,* 32-47.

Steiner, I. D. (1972). *Group process and productivity.* New York: Academic Press.

Steinfield, C. W. (1986). Computer-mediated communication in an organizational setting: Explaining task-related and socioemotional uses. In M. L. McLaughlin (Ed.), *Communication yearbook* (Vol. 9, pp. 777-804). Beverly Hills, CA: Sage.

Steinfield, C. W., & Fulk, J. (1987). On the role of theory in research on information technologies in organizations: An introduction to the special issue. *Communication Research, 14,* 479-490.

Straus, S. (1991). *Does the medium matter: An investigation of process, performance and affect in computer-mediated and face-to-face groups.* Unpublished doctoral dissertation, University of Illinois, Urbana-Champaign.

Sutherland, D., & Crosslin, R. (1989). Group decision support systems: Factors in a software implementation. *Information and Management, 16,* 93-103.

Swanson, E. B. (1986). Information systems in organization theory: A review. In R. J. Boland & R. Hirschheim (Eds.), *Critical issues in information systems research.* Chichester, UK: Wiley.

Tombari, M. L., Fitzpatrick, S. J., & Childress, W. (1985). Using computers as contingency managers in self-monitoring interventions: A case study. *Computers in Human Behavior, 1,* 75-82.

Trevino, L. K., Lengel, R. H., & Daft, R. L. (1987). Media symbolism, media richness, and media choice in organizations: A symbolic interactionist perspective. *Communication Research, 14,* 553-574.

Trice, A. W., & Treacy, M. E. (1988, Fall/Winter). Utilization as a dependent variable in MIS research. *Data Base,* pp. 33-41.

Turoff, M., & Hiltz, S. R. (1982). Computer support for group versus individual decisions. *IEEE Transactions on Communications, COM-20(1),* 82-91.

Tyran, C. K., Dennis, A. R., & Vogel, D. (1992). The application of electronic meeting technology to support strategic management. *MIS Quarterly, 16,* 313-334.

Ugbah, S. D., & Dewine, S. (1989). New communication technologies: The impact on intra-organizational dynamics. *Information and Management, 17,* 181-186.

Valacich, J. S., Dennis, A. R., & Connolly, T. (in press). Idea generation in computer-based groups: A new ending to an old story. *Organizational Behavior and Human Decision Processes.*

Valacich, J. S., Dennis, A. R., & Nunamaker, J. F. (1991a). Electronic meeting support: The groupsystems concept. *International Journal on Man-Machine Studies, 34,* 261-282.

Valacich, J. S., Dennis, A. R., & Nunamaker, J. F. (1991b). Group size and anonymity effects on computer-mediated idea generation. *Small Group Research, 23(1),* 49-73.

Valacich, J. S., Paranka, D., George, J. F., & Nunamaker, J. F. (in press). Communication concurrency and the new media: A new dimension for media richness. *Communication Research.*

Vallee, J., Johansen, R., Lipinski, H., & Wislon, T. (1977). *Group communication through computers* (Vol. 4). Menlo Park, CA: Institute for the Future.

Van de Ven, A. H., & Delbecq, A. (1974). The effectiveness of nominal, delphi, and interacting group decision making processes. *Academy of Management Journal, 17,* 605-621.

Vogel, D. R., & Nunamaker, J. (1988, September). Health service group use of automated planning support. *Administrative Radiology.*

Vogel, D. R., & Nunamaker, J. F. (1990). Design and assessment of a group decision support system. In J. Galegher, R. Kraut, & C. Egido (Eds.), *Intellectual teamwork: Social and technological foundations of cooperative work* (pp. 511-528). Hillsdale, NJ: Lawrence Erlbaum.

Vogel, D. R., Nunamaker, J. F., George, J., & Dennis, A. R. (1988). Group decision support systems: Evolution and status at the University of Arizona. In R. M. Lee, A. M. McCosh, & P. Migliarese (Eds.), *Organizational decision support systems* (pp. 287-304). North Holland: Elsevier.

Wagner, G. R. (Ed.). (1990). *Computer-augmented teamwork: A guided tour.* New York: Van Nostrand Reinhold.

Walther, J. B. (1992a). Interpersonal effects in computer-mediated interaction: A relational perspective. *Communication Research, 19,* 52-90.

Walther, J. B. (1992b). A longitudinal experiment on relational tone in computer-mediated and face-to-face interaction. In J. F. Nunamaker & R. H. Sprague (Eds.), *Proceedings of the Hawaii International Conference on System Sciences 1992* (Vol. 4, pp. 220-231). Los Alamitos, CA: IEEE Computer Society Press.

Walther, J. B., & Burgoon, J. K. (1992). Relational communication in computer-mediated interaction. *Human Communication Research, 19*(1), 50-88.

Watson, R., DeSanctis, G., & Poole, M. (1988). Using a GDSS to facilitate group consensus: Some intended and unintended consequences. *MIS Quarterly, 12,* 463-478.

Weeks, G. D., & Chapanis, A. (1976). Cooperative vs. competitive problem solving in three telecommunication modes. *Perceptual and Motor Skills, 42,* 879-917.

Wegner, D. M. (1986). Transactive memory: A contemporary analysis of the group mind. In B. Mullen & G. R. Goethals (Eds.), *Theories of group behavior* (pp. 185-208). New York: Springer.

Weill, P., & Olson, M. H. (1989). An assessment of the contingency theory of management information systems. *Journal of Management Information Systems, 6*(1), 59-85.

Weisband, S. (1992). Group discussion and first advocacy effects in computer-mediated and face-to-face decision making groups. *Organizational Behavior and Human Decision Processes, 53,* 352-380.

Williams, E. (1975). Medium or message: Communication medium as determinant of interpersonal evaluation. *Sociometry, 38,* 119-130.

Williams, E. (1977). Experimental comparisons of face-to-face and mediated communication: A review. *Psychological Bulletin, 84,* 963-976.

Williams, F., Rice, R., & Rogers, E. (1988). *Research methods and the new media.* New York: Free Press.

Yankelovich, N., Haan, B. J., Meyrowitz, N. K., & Drucker, S. M. (1988). Intermedia: The concept and the construction of a seamless information environment. *Computer, 21,* 81-94.

Zahn, G. L. (1991). Face-to-face communication in an office setting. *Communication Research, 18*(6), 737-754.

Zenger, T. R., & Lawrence, B. S. (1989). Organizational demography: The differential effects of age and tenure distributions on technical communication. *Academy of Management Journal, 32*(2), 353-376.

Zigurs, I., DeSanctis, G., & Billingsley, J. (1991). Adoption patterns and attitudinal development in computer-supported meetings: An exploratory study with SAMM. *Journal of Management Information Systems, 7*(4), 51-70.

Zigurs, I., Poole, M., & DeSanctis, G. (1988). A study of influence in computer-mediated group decision making. *MIS Quarterly, 12,* 625-644.

Annotated Bibliography of Research Literature on Electronic Technology in Work Groups

Adelman, L. (1984). Real time computer support for decision analysis in a group setting: Another class of decision support systems. *Interfaces, 14,* 75-83.

A case study of one work group using a GDSS on a project planning task (planning, idea generation, and decision making) found that all group members evaluated the quality of the decision and decision process favorably. Group members found the GDSS procedure to be effective. (There was no within-group or between-group comparison.) The decision was put into effect within 1 week after the GDSS session.

Arunachalam, V. (in press). Computer-mediated communication and structured interaction in transfer pricing negotiation. *Journal of Information Systems.*

This laboratory experiment examined the effects of communication channels and interaction structure on the outcomes of group negotiations. The design was a 2 × 2 factorial. The two levels of communication channels were face-to-face and synchronous computer conference; the two levels of interaction structure were no formal structure and a modified Nominal Group Technique. Accounting students were randomly assigned into 60 three-person groups (15 groups in each of the four conditions) and worked on three integrative bargaining tasks with logrolling potential.

Results showed that computer-mediated groups and unstructured groups obtained lower outcomes, distributed resources more unequally, deviated more from the integrative agreement, and maintained more inaccurate perceptions of the interaction than face-to-face groups. Computer-mediated groups displayed more competitive flaming behavior and a greater tendency to reach coalitional agreements than face-to-face groups. Computer-mediated groups and structured groups took more time to reach agreement than face-to-face groups and unstructured groups. On the first two problems, computer-mediated unstructured groups obtained the lowest outcomes, followed by computer-mediated structured groups, face-to-face unstructured groups, and face-to-face structured groups. On the third and final problem, face-to-face structured groups continued to obtain the highest outcomes, followed by computer-mediated structured groups, face-to-face unstructured, and computer-mediated unstructured groups. There were significant learning effects in all conditions, although computer-mediated structured groups displayed a higher rate of learning than any of the other groups, particularly in the last session.

Bui, T., Sivansankaran, T., Fijol, Y., & Woodburg, M. (1987). Identifying organizational opportunities for GDSS use: Some experimental evidence. *Transactions of Seventh Conference on Decision Support Systems* (pp. 68-75). San Francisco, CA.

   This laboratory study compared three-person groups working via computer on an idea generation task in two locations: in a decision room or dispersed. There were six groups in each of the two conditions. Results showed no differences in number of solutions or satisfaction between the two conditions; however, dispersed groups had better solutions and made faster decisions.

Chidambaram, L., Bostrom, R. P., & Wynne, B. E. (1991). The impact of GDSS on group development. *Journal of Management Information Systems, 7*(3), 3-25.

   This laboratory experiment examined the effects of computer support on the development of decision-making groups. A two-factorial repeated measures design was used, computer support (GDSS—GroupSystems or no GDSS—manual). Each of the 28 groups in the two treatment conditions was given four different tasks—one per session—at intervals of 1 week. The four tasks were business case analyses that involved strategic decision making without "correct" answers. Undergraduate business students were randomly assigned to five-person groups and the groups were randomly assigned to treatments.
   Manual groups had a higher degree of cohesiveness and were better at managing conflict than GDSS groups initially. However, this pattern reversed itself in the third and fourth sessions. As the 4-week experiment progressed, GDSS groups became more cohesive and managed conflict better than manual groups.

Connolly, T., Jessup, L. M., & Valacich, J. S. (1989). Effects of anonymity and evaluative tone on idea generation in computer-mediated groups. *Management Science, 36,* 689-703.

This experiment examined the effects of anonymity and evaluative tone on computer-mediated groups using a group decision support system to perform an idea-generation task. Advanced undergraduate business students were randomly assigned into four-person groups. (Each four-person group was composed of three naive participants and one confederate.) The 2 × 2 factorial design consisted of (a) anonymity—anonymous versus identified group members; and (b) evaluative tone of comments from the confederate group member—supportive versus critical. There were six groups in each of the four experimental conditions.

Groups with a critical confederate generated more solutions than groups with a supportive confederate, and groups whose members were anonymous generated more ideas than did groups whose members were identified. However, members of groups with a supportive confederate were more satisfied with their group process than members of groups with a critical confederate.

Daly, B. (1993). The influence of face-to-face versus computer-mediated communication channels on collective induction. *Accounting, Management & Information Technology, 3*(1), 1-22.

This study compared groups working face-to-face to groups working via computer on an intellective task. Undergraduate commerce majors were randomly assigned into four-person groups and worked on a rule induction task. A between-subjects random block design was used: Half of the groups communicated face-to-face and the other half communicated via computer network. Thirty-two four-person groups were run in each of the two conditions.

The results showed that, although there was no difference between the two conditions in the number of correct solutions, computer groups made more errors. Computer-mediated groups took longer than those in the face-to-face condition to finish the task. Members of computer-mediated groups had more equal participation rates. In addition, face-to-face groups generated more comments and were generally more positive in their responses about the task and interaction on a post-session questionnaire. Members of computer groups reported being more anxious and nervous during the experiment than members of face-to-face groups.

Dennis, A., Heminger, A., Nunamaker, J., & Vogel, D. (1990). Bringing automated support to large groups: The Burr-Brown experience. *Information and Management, 18*(3), 111-121.

This case study described the use of a group decision support system by a large group for strategic planning. Burr-Brown used the system developed at the University of Arizona MIS Department to carry out its annual strategic planning meeting. The 31 participants in the meeting were all senior managers at the division manager level and above. Measures of effectiveness, efficiency, and user satisfaction all indicated that the system provided intended group support during the 3-day planning session. The meeting was seen as effective and efficient. Users reported a high level of satisfaction with the system. (There was no within-group or between-group comparison.)

DeSanctis, G., Poole, M. S., Lewis, H., & Desharnais, G. (1991). Using computing in quality team meetings: Initial observations from the IRS-Minnesota Project. *Journal of Management Information Systems, 8*(3), 7-26.

   This study presents some initial findings on the extent and types of uses of GDSS technology made by 10 quality teams at the Internal Revenue Service during the first 7 months of a multiyear study. Five "new" teams had the GDSS technology (SAMM) available to them since their initial formation. Two "older" teams were introduced to SAMM during the last few months of their participation in the quality process and 3 were introduced to SAMM in the middle of their life. The analysis is based on 136 SAMM-supported meetings. Teams who were introduced to SAMM later in their life were less likely to use the technology in their meetings and tended to stick with basic Level 1 uses. Teams who were introduced to SAMM in the early or middle part of their life were much more likely to use the technology in their meetings and to use the advanced Level 2 structures. Groups tended to use the system for task- or process-related activities. Self-reports of satisfaction with the technology were high on average. (No within-group or between-group comparison was made.)

Dickson, G., Lee, J., Robinson, L., & Heath, R. (1989). Observations on GDSS interaction: Chauffeured, facilitated, and user-driven systems. In R. Blanning & D. King (Eds.), *Proceedings of the 22nd annual Hawaii International Conference on System Sciences* (Vol. 3, pp. 337-343). Los Alamitos, CA: IEEE Computer Society Press.

   This study investigated the outcomes of the use of Group Decision Support Systems (GDSS) under three modes of user interaction: Chauffeured GDSS (person from meeting room took orders from group and implemented them); facilitator driven (facilitator imposed decision-making process on group); and user driven (each group member interacted freely with GDSS). All groups worked on a judgmental task. Results showed that chauffeured and facilitated groups achieved higher degrees of consensus than did user-driven groups.

Dubrovsky, V. J., Kiesler, S., & Sethna, B. N. (1991). The equalization phenomenon: Status effects in computer-mediated and face-to-face decision-making groups. *Human-Computer Interaction, 6,* 119-146.

   This lab experiment examined the effects of electronic mail on the decisions of groups with members that differed in social status. Ninety-six students (60 male, 36 female) participated in this study. Twenty-four were enrolled in the graduate MBA program; 72 were college freshman. All participated in four-person same-sex decision-making groups. Each group was composed of three low-status (freshman) and one high-status (MBA student) member. Twenty-four, four-person groups discussed and came to consensus on four decision (choice shift) tasks. Two of the four decision tasks concerned career choices of college graduates; two concerned freshman curriculum. Group members worked on two tasks while communicating face-to-face, and two tasks while separated and communicating through electronic mail.

When groups made decisions in face-to-face meetings, the high-status member dominated the discussions and influenced the decisions made. When the same groups made comparable decisions using electronic mail, status inequalities were significantly reduced; participation and influence in groups were more equal across social status. There were more instances of uninhibited remarks when groups communicated by electronic mail rather than face-to-face.

Easton, G., George, J., Nunamaker, J., & Pendergast, M. (1990). Using two different electronic meeting system tools for the same task: An experimental comparison. *Journal of Management Information Systems, 7*(1), 85-100.

This study compared the quality and quantity of ideas generated by groups using two different electronic meeting system tools. The first system, Electronic Brainstorming System (EBS), used three tools in a specified order: electronic brainstorming, issue analyzer, and voting. The second system, Electronic Discussion System (EDS), was a single tool that incorporated the same three functions. The main difference between the two systems was that the first was a multifile system in that each member did not have access to all other members' ideas at once; each file was randomly distributed, so members may or may not have seen all of the files of other members. EDS allowed all members access to all comments in "real time."

Sixty undergraduates participated in this study. Five groups of six undergraduates worked on an idea-generation task in each of the two decision system conditions.

Decision quality was better for groups using EDS, although groups using the separate tools generated more ideas. There were no statistically significant differences between the two conditions for satisfaction with process or degree of consensus among group members.

Eveland, J. D., & Bikson, T. K. (1989). Work group structures and computer support: A field experiment. *ACM Transactions on Office Information Systems, 6*, 354-379.

This field experiment compared two task forces composed of about 40 retirees and workers of an organization. One task force communicated via an asynchronous computer network exclusively, the other had no communication restrictions (standard group). Results showed that the electronic task force had broader participation and a fluctuating leadership pattern. The standard task force had fewer participants contributing on a regular basis, greater centralization, and more stable leadership. The electronic task force reported more satisfaction with the process.

Finholt, T., Sproull, L., & Kiesler, S. (1990). Communication and performance in ad hoc groups. In J. Galegher, R. Kraut, & C. Egido (Eds.), *Intellectual teamwork: Social and technological foundations of cooperative work* (pp. 291-326). Hillsdale, NJ: Lawrence Erlbaum.

This study examined the effects of electronic mail on the performance of ad hoc groups. Seven software development teams were formed in a required upper division information systems course. Each of the seven teams consisted of two managers and from five to eight programmers and documenters. Each team was assigned a different software development project for an actual client. The team task was to design, build, and test a working system to the client's specification and satisfaction within a period of 3 months.

Data included (a) background information on each participant (GPA, number of computer classes taken, etc.); (b) questionnaires administered at the beginning and end of the 3-month period; (c) observations of face-to-face meetings in each team at 1-month intervals; (d) participants' reports of phone calls, memos, computer mail, and face-to-face interaction with other team members; and (e) client and course instructor ratings of group and individual final performance. The initial questionnaire contained items to assess likely level of participation in the group. The final questionnaire contained scales to measure commitment to the group, quality of communication, and perceived quality of coordination within the group.

Results suggested that a computer mail system contributed to the productivity of ad hoc task groups. In general, groups that used a computer mail system more not only outperformed groups that did not, but spent less time in meetings and used other kinds of communication less.

Gallupe, R. B., Bastianutti, L. M., & Cooper, W. H. (1991). Unblocking brainstorms. *Journal of Applied Psychology, 76*(1), 137-142.

Nominal and interacting groups using electronic and nonelectronic communication were compared in a 2×2 factorial design. Business and commerce students were randomly assigned to four-person same-sex groups and worked on an idea generation task ("thumbs" problem). There were 10 groups in each of the four conditions. All participants in the electronic conditions entered their ideas into computers. In the electronic interactive groups, ideas were entered by individuals and stored by the group. One idea appeared in the bottom portion of the screen and random samples of the ideas produced by the group appeared in the top half of the screen. The ideas entered by subjects in electronic nominal groups were simply stored in each participant's computers. In the structured face-to-face (manual) conditions, interacting groups verbalized their ideas to the other members of the group. Individuals in the face-to-face nominal condition wrote their ideas on paper without communicating those ideas to others.

The findings indicated that electronic groups generated significantly more nonredundant ideas than did manual groups, but the productivity of nominal and interacting groups did not differ. In contrast, interacting groups reported feeling more motivated to generate quality ideas, feeling more comfortable with the idea generation process, feeling a greater opportunity to express their ideas, and feeling that they had generated more ideas than they actually had generated. Electronic groups also found the task easier than did face-to-face groups.

Gallupe, R. B., Dennis, A. R., Cooper, W. H., Valacich, J. S., Bastianutti, L. M., & Nunamaker, J. F. (1992). Electronic brainstorming and group size. *Academy of Management Journal, 35,* 350-369.

This study examined the effects of group size on the idea generation of groups using electronic versus face-to-face communication on a brainstorming task. Two experiments were conducted with groups of varying size: One study compared 2-, 4-, and 6-person groups and the other compared 6- and 12-person groups. The participants in the two studies were undergraduate students enrolled in business courses. The two studies were conducted at different universities. The researchers employed a within-group design with counterbalanced order of conditions in both studies. The two independent variables were group size and brainstorming technology (computer vs. manual). The participants were randomly assigned into groups of varying sizes and worked together on two idea generation tasks. Groups used the computer brainstorming technique for one task and the manual brainstorming technique for the other.

In the first study, computer groups produced significantly more nonredundant ideas than manual groups in 4- and 6-member groups, but not in the 2-member groups. The same pattern emerged for the quality of ideas: Computer groups had a higher overall quality score and generated more high-quality ideas than the manual groups in 4- and 6-member groups, but not in the 2-member groups. Computer groups perceived less production blocking than manual groups and the effect was more pronounced in larger groups than in smaller groups. Computer groups perceived less evaluation apprehension than manual groups. Perceptions of satisfaction in the 2-person groups were not significantly different across media, but satisfaction decreased as groups became larger. The 6-member nonelectronic brainstorming groups reported less satisfaction than the 6-member electronic brainstorming groups. These findings were replicated in the second study for 6- versus 12-member groups.

Gallupe, R. B., DeSanctis, G., & Dickson, G. (1988). Computer-based support for group problem solving: An experimental investigation. *MIS Quarterly, 12,* 277-296.

This experiment examined the effects of use of a GDSS technology on group decision quality and individual perceptions within a problem-finding context. The design was 2×2 factorial: (a) GDSS support (supported vs. nonsupported) and (b) task difficulty (difficult vs. less difficult). Seventy-two undergraduate business administration students were randomly assigned to three-person groups and worked on one of two versions of a crisis management task. Groups were not given a time limit for completing the task. There were six groups in each of the four conditions.

GDSS groups generated more alternatives and had better quality decisions (as compared to decisions made by "experts") on both high- and low-difficulty tasks, but took longer to make decisions than face-to-face groups. Face-to-face groups reported more confidence in their decisions, more satisfaction with the decision process, higher agreement among members on the final decision, and less conflict in their group discussions.

Gallupe, R. B., & McKeen, J. (1990). Enhancing computer-mediated communication: An experimental study into the use of a decision support system for face-to-face versus remote meetings. *Information and Management, 18,* 1-13.

This experiment examined the effects of physical proximity and decision structure on the quality of group decisions and user reactions for groups working via computer. Fifty-four undergraduate business administration students were randomly assigned into 20 three-person decision-making groups and into four experimental conditions: (a) in a decision room with GDSS structure; (b) in a decision room without structure; (c) dispersed with structure; or (d) dispersed without structure. DECAID1, developed by Gallupe and McKeen, provided the basic functions of recording, storing, organizing, and displaying alternatives that were entered by group members, aggregating and displaying preference rankings for those alternatives, and recording votes for the various alternatives generated for groups in the GDSS conditions. There were five groups in each of the two GDSS treatments and four groups in the two non-GDSS treatments.

The results showed no significant between-group differences in decision quality. GDSS groups took longer than unstructured groups to reach a decision; dispersed groups took longer than proximate. Groups in the remote setting were significantly less satisfied with their decision process than those in the face-to-face setting.

George, J., Easton, G., Nunamaker, J., & Northcraft, G. (1990). A study of collaborative group work with and without computer-based support. *Information Systems Research, 1*(4), 394-415.

This experiment examined the effects of communication medium, assigned leadership and anonymity on group process and outcomes on an idea generation/intellective task. An incomplete $2 \times 2 \times 2$ factorial design was constructed by varying (a) communication medium (GDSS vs. manual); (b) leadership (assigned vs. emergent); and (c) anonymity (identified vs. anonymous); but excluding the two anonymous manual communication conditions from the factorial design. Five six-person groups of upper-level MIS undergraduates were randomly assigned to each of the remaining six conditions.

There were no significant differences between conditions for decision quality or number of unique alternatives. GDSS groups were less likely to reach consensus, took more time to reach a decision, and had more equal levels of member participation than manual groups. No main effects were found for leadership or anonymity conditions.

Hiltz, S. R., Johnson, K., & Turoff, M. (1986). Experiments in group decision making, 1: Communications process and outcome in face-to-face vs. computerized conferences. *Human Communication Research, 13*(2), 225-252.

This study investigated the effects of computer mediation on the process and performance of decision-making groups. The design was a 2 × 2 factorial. The two modes of communication were face-to-face and synchronous computer conferences; the two types of tasks were judgmental and intellective. Undergraduates were randomly assigned into 32 five-person groups.

Results showed that computer groups had less total communication, proportionately more task-oriented communication, and more equal participation; and were less likely to reach agreement. There were no differences between communication modes for decision quality.

Hiltz, S. R., Johnson, K., & Turoff, M. (1991). Group decision support: The effects of designated human leaders and statistical feedback in computerized conferences. *Journal of Management Information Systems, 8,* 81-108.

This study investigated the effects of a designated leader and of statistical feedback in computerized conferences. Twenty-four five-person groups consisting of professionals and managers (six groups in each of four conditions) used a computer synchronous conferencing system to reach agreement on the best solution to a complex ranking problem (Lost in the Arctic). A 2 × 2 factorial design was constructed by varying designated leadership (designated leader or no leader) and statistical feedback (present or absent). Groups with designated leadership (DL) used software support to elect a discussion leader. Groups with statistical feedback (SF) were presented periodically with tables that displayed the mean rank and degree of consensus for each item.

Designated leadership tended to improve the quality of decisions, but the differences were statistically significant only for the "collective intelligence" measure (the degree to which groups perform better than the individual members). Designated leadership tended to improve levels of agreement, but the differences were not significant. Designated leadership did not improve subjective satisfaction. Statistical feedback tended to be detrimental to the quality of group decisions and did not significantly improve group agreement or subjective satisfaction. Statistical feedback was associated with fewer text comments and more rerankings of items by the participants. The authors examined group composition in their analyses and concluded that cooperative groups composed of members with previous experience using computers may be good candidates for using computerized conferences for discussion and decision making.

Hiltz, S. R., Turoff, M., & Johnson, K. (1988). Experiments in group decision making, 3: Disinhibition, deindividuation, and group process in pen name and real name computer conferences. *Decision Support Systems, 5*, 1-16.

This field experiment focused on the effect of using pen names (a form of anonymity) in computer conferences for group decision making. The subjects were peer groups of managers in a large corporation with a well-developed "corporate culture." Groups worked on three choice dilemma tasks. Six five-member groups were run in each of three conditions: face-to-face, identified computer conference, and pen name computer conference.

Pen name conferences (versus face-to-face) showed consistent, but statistically insignificant tendencies toward disagreement about the final group choice, more participation, and more equal participation. Choices made by groups in the pen name condition tended to be more conservative. There was very little uninhibited behavior in any of the groups. The authors concluded that problem-solving techniques using software structures that employ forms of anonymity appeared to be helpful options in future group decision support systems built within computer-mediated communication systems.

Ho, T. H., & Raman, K. S. (1991). The effects of GDSS and elected leadership on small group meetings. *Journal of Management Information Systems, 8*, 109-134.

This study investigated the effects of a group decision support system and elected leadership on meetings of five-person groups. A 3×2 factorial design crossed decision support (no support, manual support, and GDSS support) with elected leadership (yes or no). Forty-eight undergraduate student groups were randomly assigned to one of the six experimental conditions. The groups solved a preference task that required resolution of competing preference structures.

Manual groups displayed a significantly higher postmeeting consensus than did GDSS groups. Elected leadership had no significant effect on postmeeting consensus. Groups that had high premeeting consensus seemed willing to let one member dominate the discussion. There were no significant main effects for equality of influence, although there was a significant negative correlation between equality of influence and premeeting consensus in GDSS groups. This relation was not present in manual or baseline groups.

Hollingshead, A. B. (1993). *Information, influence and technology in group decision making*. Unpublished doctoral dissertation, University of Illinois, Urbana-Champaign.

An experiment examined the effects of communication media, group decision task, and access to information on the pooling of individually held information and on the quality of group decisions. A $2 \times 2 \times 2$ between-subjects factorial design was constructed by varying (a) communication media (face-to-face vs. synchronous computer conference); (b) decision task (choose best vs. rank order); (c) degree of information access during the group decision (no access vs. complete information access). Undergraduate psychology students were randomly assigned to three-person groups and to the eight conditions. There were 10 groups in each condition. Each group made a financial investment decision in which one investment alternative was objectively better than the others, and in which information sharing was required to discover which was the better alternative.

Results were consistent with past research: Groups generally did not select the objectively optimal company for investment and the information presented during the group discussion focused on members' prediscussion preferences. However, there was a significant Group Decision Task × Communication Media interaction for decision quality. Groups in the face-to-face rank order conditions were most likely to discover the better alternative. In addition, there were differences in the decision process between the two media. Face-to-face groups made significantly more comments and took a significantly shorter time to reach consensus than did computer groups. There was a significantly higher proportion of normative influence attempts, a significantly lower proportion of informational influence acts, a significantly lower proportion of speculation, and a significantly higher proportion of socioemotional communication in the computer-mediated condition than in the face-to-face condition.

Hollingshead, A. B., McGrath, J. E., & O'Connor, K. M. (1993). Group task performance and communication technology: A longitudinal study of computer-mediated vs face-to-face work groups. *Small Group Research*, 24(3), 307-333.

This article explored the effects of computer-mediated communication and task type on group task performance, testing predictions from two models. The first model ("Task as Moderator") predicted that the type of task on which the group is working would moderate the effects of communication medium on task performance over time. The second model ("Change as Moderator") predicted that cumulative experience, on the one hand, and certain kinds of changes imposed on the group, on the other hand, would moderate these effects.

Participants were enrolled in an advanced undergraduate psychology course. Twenty-two groups ranging from three to five members worked on a different task for a 2-hour period each week for a total of 13 weeks. The 13 tasks consisted of 3 generating plans tasks, 6 intellective tasks, 2 decision-making tasks, and 2 negotiation tasks. One half of the groups were assigned to work together on the tasks through a synchronous computer conferencing system; the other half were assigned to work on the tasks face-to-face. For the 7th and 8th weeks of the semester, all 22 groups switched communication media—so the computer groups worked face-to-face and the face-to-face groups worked on the computer. The groups switched back to their original media on the 9th week and continued working in that communication medium through the end of the semester.

Providing newly formed groups with computers for intragroup communication had detrimental effects on group task performance initially, but within a relatively short period of time—3 weeks—there were no significant differences in task performance between face-to-face and computer-mediated groups. When groups that had developed as face-to-face groups were assigned to a computer-mediated condition during the 6th and 7th weeks of the study, they experienced similar detrimental effects on their task performance. These results suggest that the newness of the medium, and not the newness of the group, led to poorer task performance for computer groups in some weeks.

Although there were no differences in performance between computer groups and face-to-face groups for generate and decision-making tasks, face-to-face groups performed better on negotiation and intellective tasks than did their computer-mediated counterparts. The results supported all of the predictions of the second (change) model and only partially supported predictions of the first (task effects) model.

Jarvenpaa, S. L., Rao, R. S., and Huber, G. P. (1988). Computer support for meetings of medium-sized groups working on unstructured problems: A field experiment. *MIS Quarterly, 12,* 645-665.

This experiment examined the consequences of adding computer support for teams working on unstructured, high-level conceptual software design problems in face-to-face groups. Three teams of seven software designers performed unstructured, high-level conceptual software design tasks that involved generating ideas and reaching consensus on the best ideas. A 3 × 3 repeated measures Graeco-Latin Square design was used, with three forms of communication media (conventional, electronic blackboard, networked workstations) and each team worked with one of the meeting technologies for three sequential 1-hour sessions for a total of nine sessions.

Decision quality was best for groups communicating via electronic blackboard (EBB), second best for networked groups, and worst for face-to-face groups. There were no differences in equality of participation, perceived equity of participation or satisfaction with process for the three conditions. Face-to-face groups without electronic support had the highest level of communication thoroughness (followed by EBB-supported, then workstation-supported meetings). EBB had higher levels of group attention and greater focus on completing the task.

Jessup, L. M., Connolly, T., & Galegher, J. (1990). The effects of anonymity on GDSS group process with an idea-generating task. *MIS Quarterly*, 14, 312-321.

This experiment examined the effects of anonymity on the idea generation in groups using a group decision support system (Plex Center GDSS). The study compared anonymous versus identified four-person groups of undergraduate business students communicating via computer network. A total of 20 groups participated in the study.

Anonymous groups generated more comments overall, more solution clarifications, more critical comments, and more questions about solutions. Anonymity had no significant effect on the number of solutions or number of supportive comments.

Jessup, L. M., & Tansik, D. A. (1991). Group problem solving in an automated environment: The effects of anonymity and proximity on group process and outcome with a group decision support system. *Decision Sciences*, 22(2), 266-279.

A laboratory experiment examined the effects of anonymity and proximity on group process and outcome with a group decision support system. Using a 2 × 2 factorial design, the researchers compared anonymous or identified four-person groups of undergraduate business students working either in proximity or dispersed on an idea generation task using an electronic brainstorming program from Plex Center. Five groups were run in each of the four cells for a total of 20 groups.

The number of solutions was greatest in the anonymous/dispersed condition and least in the identified/proximate condition. The most satisfied groups were in the anonymous/dispersed and identified/proximate conditions.

Kiesler, S., Zubrow, D., Moses, A. M., & Geller, V. (1985). Affect in computer-mediated communication: An experiment in synchronous terminal-to-terminal discussion. *Human Computer Interaction*, 1, 77-104.

This study examined the effects of communication media and anxiety level on the acquaintance process in dyads. Eighty male and female undergraduates who did not know each other were randomly assigned to same-sex dyads and discussed a series of questions to get to know each other. Ten pairs of subjects were randomly assigned to each of four conditions in a 2 × 2 factorial design, varying anxiety evaluation level (low, high) and communication medium (face-to-face, synchronous computer conference).

Computer-mediated communication influenced the development of new interpersonal relationships: Subjects evaluated each other less positively and they were more uninhibited in their comments. But becoming acquainted with someone through the computer, rather than face-to-face, had no significant effect on physiological arousal, emotions, or self-evaluations. These findings suggest that computer-mediated communication, rather than provoking emotionality per se, elicits asocial or unregulated behavior.

Lea, M., & Spears, R. (1991). Computer-mediated communication, de-individuation, and group decision making. *International Journal of Man-Machine Studies, 34,* 283-301.

This experiment examined social psychological processes in computer-mediated group decision making. The authors noted prior findings, that groups communicating via computer produce more polarized decisions than face-to-face groups. They proposed an alternative model to account for those findings, based on social identity theory and a reconceptualization of deindividuation that takes into account social and normative factors associated with group polarization.

Computer-mediated (via electronic mail) individual decisions on four controversial issues before and after group discussion were examined. Forty-eight participants (from a volunteer subject panel of first-year psychology students) were randomly assigned into three-person groups, and into four conditions within a 2 × 2 factorial design that varied: (a) the salience of either the group or individual identity of participants; and (b) the physical location of group members: dispersed or proximate. The dependent variable measures were the attitudinal position of each member for each of the four issues before and after group discussion, and the quantity and content of participation.

The authors discussed results only for comparison between the group and individual salience conditions for the dispersed groups. Participants in the group salience condition were significantly more polarized in the direction of the group norm than participants in the individual salience condition. Greater polarization was associated with the exchange of significantly fewer words, shorter messages, and a smaller proportion of remarks related to the discussion topic. In addition, members participated more unequally, exchanged more social remarks and perceived least disagreement among themselves after the discussions in the group salience condition than in the individual salience condition.

McGuire, T. W., Kiesler, S., & Siegel, J. (1987). Group and computer-mediated discussion effects in risk decision making. *Journal of Personality and Social Psychology, 52,* 917-930.

This study examined the effects of computer-mediation on the influence processes in group decisions. Managers made multiattribute risk choices (two investment alternatives, each with multiple outcomes) individually and in 16 three-person groups. Two group decisions were reached during face-to-face discussion and two were reached during computer-mediated discussion. Multiattribute risk choices and member attitudes in face-to-face groups after face-to-face discussion were risk averse for gains and risk-seeking for losses, a tendency predicted by prospect theory and consistent with choice shift research. In contrast, the group decisions during computer-mediated discussions did not shift in the direction of prospect theory predictions. The results were consistent with persuasive arguments theory that suggests that computer-mediated discussion contains less argumentation than face-to-face discussion.

McLeod, P. L., & Liker, J. K. (1992). Electronic meeting systems: Evidence from a low structure environment. *Information Systems Research, 3*(3), 195-223.

This study investigated the effects of computer support on the interpersonal and task processes, performance, and member satisfaction in decision-making groups. Thirty-four groups of four or five students from organizational behavior classes worked on two different tasks presented in the same order. The first task was an intellective ranking task; the second was a decision-making, in-basket task. Both tasks required groups to reach consensus: On the proper sequence of activities for planning, organizing, implementing, and controlling a hypothetical project for the first task, and on the response for each piece of correspondence for the second task. Groups were assigned randomly to either the computer-supported GDSS (capture lab) condition or the manually supported face-to-face communication condition (group members were supplied with paper and a common writing space) to work on each task.

There were no significant between-subject differences in equality of participation. Computer-supported groups showed a higher concentration of task-oriented behavior. Computer-supported groups performed better on the intellective task than the manual groups, but performed worse than the manual groups on the decision-making task. The manual groups wrote responses that were longer and more completely formatted and that showed a greater awareness of underlying problems on the decision-making task. There were no significant differences in satisfaction between the computer-supported and manual groups for the intellective task, although the manual groups reported higher levels of satisfaction on the appropriateness of their task strategies.

Nunamaker, J., Vogel, D., Heminger, A., Martz, B., Grohowski, R., & McGoff, C. (1989). Experiences at IBM with group support systems: A field study. *Decision Support Systems: The International Journal, 5*(2), 183-196.

The results of a GDSS field study conducted at an IBM site in New York are presented in this article. Groups participated on a voluntary basis and participants ranged from the plant manager and high-level executives to shop floor personnel. Group size ranged from 4 to 10 members with an average size of 8. Data from 387 group members were collected. Work groups brought their problems with them. The problem domains included requirements analysis, strategic planning, and resource allocation. The GDSS technology provided to the groups consisted of three linked software tools: an electronic brainstorming tool that supported idea generation, an issue analyzer tool that helped group members identify and consolidate key focus items resulting from idea generation, and a voting tool that provided a variety of prioritizing methods.

There was strong agreement among participants that the system did provide process effectiveness. In terms of efficiency, man-hours were saved in every case recorded, with an average-per-session saving of 55.51% (based on estimates of the time it would have taken via face-to-face interaction). Users reported being very satisfied with the system. Participation within each group seemed to be more equally distributed than in face-to-face interaction. (Note: No actual face-to-face comparison groups were run.)

Poole, M. S., & DeSanctis, G. (1992). Microlevel structuration in computer-supported group decision making. *Human Communication Research*, *19*(1), 5-49.

This study examined how groups incorporate a computerized group decision support system into their decision processes. The study focused on the effects of restrictiveness of GDSS technology on structuration processes and subsequent change in consensus.

The data were a sample of transcribed meetings of 18 groups using a GDSS (SAMM) in a face-to-face meeting. The groups were selected from a larger sample of 54 groups collected by Watson, DeSanctis, and Poole (1988). In those studies student teams of three to five people made budget allocation decisions for a philanthropic foundation. Each transcript was coded using a 31-category scheme for coding structuring (appropriation) moves that groups use when they invoke GDSS or other structures.

Groups that engaged in faithful appropriations (i.e., that used the system as designed) had greater change in consensus than those than did not. Faithful appropriation was associated with favorable outcomes. However, there were no differences between high and low consensus change groups for the amount of conflict over appropriations. Variations in the restrictiveness of the GDSS led to differences in structuration processes: Increased restrictiveness reduced structuring moves devoted to controlling the GDSS while increasing those devoted to working with system products.

Poole, M. S., Holmes, M., & DeSanctis, G. (1991). Conflict management in a computer-supported meeting environment. *Management Science*, *37*(8), 926-953.

This study examined the conflict potential and conflict management strategies of groups using various communication technologies. Groups using a GDSS (SAMM) were compared to groups using a manual version of the same decision structures that are built into SAMM, and to unsupported groups.

A subset of the data collected by Watson, DeSanctis, and Poole (1988) was analyzed. A random sample of 40 groups was selected out of the 82 three- and four-person groups for these analyses: 13 groups using a GDSS (SAMM), 13 manual groups (face-to-face with decision structure), 14 baseline groups (face-to-face without decision structure). The participants were graduate and undergraduate students enrolled in introductory management science classes. Groups performed "the foundation task," which contained a series of budget allocation decisions designed to elicit interpersonal conflict. To identify level of conflict, the researchers used the Group Working Relations Coding System (GWRCS) (Poole & Roth, 1988a). Low conflict, or the absence of conflict, was defined as periods of focused work in which members were task focused and did not disagree with each other. High conflict was defined as periods of opposition where disagreements were personalized and were expressed through the formation of opposing sides. Moderate conflict was defined as periods of critical work in which members disagreed with each other but the disagreements centered on ideas or on the group's task.

Manual and GDSS groups had significantly longer discussions than baseline groups, so proportions were used to correct for unequal session lengths. The differences between GDSS, manual, and baseline conditions suggest that structure had an effect on conflict level and conflict management behaviors but that computerization had an effect beyond structure. There were differences in the level of conflict in SAMM-supported versus manually supported and unsupported groups, and in the conflict management behaviors adopted in the different conditions. Conflict in manual groups generally remained at low or moderate levels. Conflict in GDSS groups seemed to reach high levels and then was fairly quickly reduced to moderate levels. Baseline groups had a relatively high proportion of high-level conflict and a low proportion of low-level conflict. Manual groups tended to deal with conflict in a low-key fashion that did not develop opposition between group members, although both GDSS and baseline groups surfaced conflict as open opposition between members. There was no significant difference between conditions for the outcome measure, change in consensus. GDSS groups tended to be more focused on written materials, were more likely to de-emphasize personal relations, showed more positive affect, and discussed their conflict management process more than in the other two conditions.

Sambamurthy, V., DeSanctis, G., & Poole, M. S. (in press). The effects of alternative computer-based designs on equivocality reduction during group decision-making. *Information Systems Research.*

This experiment tested the prediction, drawn from adaptive structuration theory, that group attitudes toward GDSS will directly impact group outcomes. Thirty-nine groups, comprising a total of 188 group members, were randomly assigned to one of two treatment conditions, Level 1 or Level 2 GDSS, to work on a stakeholder's decision-making task. The Level 2 GDSS contained both communication and consensus structures, whereas the Level 1 GDSS contained equivalent communication structures but limited consensus structures. The participants in this study were undergraduate majors in business and speech communication. There was some variation in the size of the groups (approximately five members).

Groups using the Level 2 GDSS achieved significantly higher levels of postmeeting convergence and reported more confidence in their recommendations than groups using the Level 1 GDSS. There were no significant differences between the two GDSS in the perceived quality of recommendations or satisfaction with the decision process. Groups that reported more positive attitudes toward GDSS also reported more confidence in their recommendations, reported more satisfaction with the decision process and with the decision outcome, and presented higher-quality recommendations.

Sambamurthy, V., & Poole, M. S. (in press). The effects of variations in capabilities of GDSS designs on management of cognitive conflict in groups. *Information Systems Research.*

This lab study examined how variations in the sophistication of computer systems affected aspects of the conflict interaction processes in groups: the degree of conflict, the productivity of conflict management, and the amount of change in consensus. The assumption that emergent conflict interaction processes in groups would mediate the influence of intervention technologies on group outcomes was tested.

Groups either used a Level 1 GDSS (providing only communication support) or a Level 2 GDSS (providing communication and decision support) on a stakeholder's task. This study analyzed a stratified random sample of data collected to compare the effects of sophistication of GDSS technologies on group outcomes without examining aspects of the group interaction process. From 40 groups in the original study, 20 were selected for this study. Ten groups used a Level 1 GDSS and 10 groups used a Level 2 GDSS. Undergraduate students enrolled in introductory management science courses worked on a stakeholder's case in which six competing strategies were presented to the group members for evaluation and selection.

The results indicated that differences in the amounts of change in consensus were related to the sophistication of GDSS technology. Groups who used the more sophisticated GDSS technology (Level 2) had more conflict that surfaced during their discussion and had a higher productivity of conflict management than the less sophisticated GDSS (Level 1). In turn, these factors enabled groups to achieve greater change in consensus.

Siegel, J., Dubrovsky, V., Kiesler, S., & McGuire, T. W. (1986). Group processes in computer-mediated communication. *Organizational Behavior & Human Decision Processes, 37,* 157-187.

This study explored the effects of computer-mediated communication on several aspects of communication behavior: (a) communication effectiveness, which refers to group members' ability to communicate data, opinions, ideas, and feelings in the most efficient manner; (b) participation of group members, which refers to the distribution of communication among members of the group; (c) interpersonal behavior, which refers to overt expressive behavior and is relevant to how a group deals with conflict; and (d) consensus development and group choice, which are reflected in a group decision.

Three experiments with repeated measures designs explored the effects of computer-mediated communication on communication efficiency, participation, interpersonal behavior, and group choice. Experiment 1 compared face-to-face versus anonymous computer interaction versus identified computer interaction. Experiment 2 compared simultaneous group communication via computer versus forced turn-taking computer-mediated communication. Experiment 3 compared face-to-face, simultaneous computer conferences, and computer mail.

Undergraduate students were randomly assigned to three-person groups. The total number of three-person groups in the three experiments was 48 (Experiment 1: 18, Experiment 2: 12, Experiment 3: 18). Groups in all three experiments worked on the same type of task: to reach consensus on choice-dilemma problems that involved selecting acceptable levels of risk for highly attractive, but risky career decisions. First, subjects privately completed a questionnaire for each of the problems they would encounter in the group; then they met in each of the communication conditions to consider one of the problems. The order of the communication media conditions was counterbalanced. The four main dependent variables were communication efficiency (time to consensus, number of remarks, task-oriented remarks, and decision proposals as a proportion of total remarks), social equalization (equal participation in group discussion), uninhibited communication, and choice shift.

Computer-mediated groups exchanged fewer remarks during group discussion, and took longer to reach consensus, than did face-to-face groups. However, computer-mediated groups and face-to-face groups were not significantly different in the proportion of task-oriented discussion, but computer groups presented proportionately more explicit decision proposals. (The frequency of decision proposals across the two media was not presented.) Members of computer-mediated groups participated more equally in group discussions than did face-to-face groups. Computer-mediated groups also exhibited more uninhibited behavior—using strong and inflammatory expressions in interpersonal interactions. Decisions of computer-mediated groups shifted further away from the members' initial individual choices compared with group decisions using face-to-face discussions. The computer technologies had essentially the same decision-making outcomes.

Smith, J., & Vanecek, M. (1988). Computer conferencing and task-oriented decisions: Implications for group decision support. *Information and Management, 14*, 123-132.

This study examined the effects of computer conferencing on group decision making. Sixty-six two-person groups worked on a complex intellective task either via a simulated conferencing system or face-to-face. Each group had 2 hours to complete the task. The participants in the study were undergraduates.

Face-to-face groups deviated less from the correct answer, shared more information, derived more correct reasons for eliminating wrong alternatives, and considered more important case attributes in their decisions than computer groups. Face-to-face groups also perceived more progress and perceived more freedom to participate.

Smith, J., & Vanecek, M. (1990). Dispersed group decision making using nonsimultaneous computer conferencing: A report of research. *Journal of Management Science, 7*(2), 71-92.

This study examined the effects of asynchronous computer conferencing (EIES) on group decision making. Seventeen five-person groups worked on a complex intellective task. Seven dispersed groups worked on the problem via an asynchronous computer network and 10 groups worked face-to-face. Each asynchronous group had 2 weeks to complete the task; the face-to-face groups met for approximately 1 hour to discuss their case verbally. The participants in the study were volunteers from professional organizations and several corporations.

Face-to-face groups shared more of the important information crucial to finding the correct solution, derived more correct reasons for eliminating wrong alternatives, and perceived more progress than computer groups. There were no significant differences between communication media for perceived freedom to participate and deviation from the correct answer.

Sproull, L. S., & Kiesler, S. (1986). Reducing social context cues: Electronic mail in organizational communication. *Management Science, 32*(11), 1492-1512.

This field study of 513 EMS users in the research and development and business products divisions of a Fortune 500 company used questionnaire data and actual messages to examine electronic mail communication at all levels of the organization. Data were collected during an 8-week period in the spring of 1983 by interview, questionnaire, and content coding of actual mail. Each participant saved a hard copy of every message sent or received for 3 days prior to a scheduled interview. Sproull and Kiesler examined participants' self-reports about attributes of specific messages, actual observed attributes of the messages, and self-reports about general electronic mail behavior and attitudes.

Findings are consistent with previous experimental studies. Decreasing social context cues had substantial deregulating effects on communication. Much of the information conveyed through electronic mail was information that would not have been conveyed through another medium. Social context cues were relatively weak in communications via electronic mail. EMS behavior was relatively self-absorbed, relatively undifferentiated by status, and relatively uninhibited and nonconforming. The authors provide three alternative explanations for these findings: technical unreliability, user inexperience, and lack of widespread access to the technology.

Steeb, R., & Johnston, S. C. (1981). A computer-based interactive system for group decision-making. *IEEE Transactions on Systems, Man, and Cybernetics, SMC-11*(8), 544-552.

This study examined the impact of a GDSS (Perceptronics' Group Decision Aid) on decision quality. The purpose of this GDSS was to guide the group decision-making process by selective elicitation of a decision tree that incorporated value and probability inputs from all group members. It was designed to identify conflicts in value judgments and to initiate discussions through use of multiattribute utility analysis. Ten three-person groups worked on a complex political crisis task either face-to-face or using the GDSS. Groups in the GDSS condition took longer to reach a decision, but made better quality decisions, and were more satisfied with the decision process and the decision itself, than were face-to-face groups.

Straus, S. (1991). *Does the medium matter: An investigation of process, performance and affect in computer-mediated and face-to-face groups.* Unpublished doctoral dissertation, University of Illinois, Urbana-Champaign.

This experiment investigated the interaction of communication media and task characteristics on group interaction, performance, and satisfaction. McGrath's (1984) framework of group tasks and Daft and Lengel's (1984, 1986) theory of information richness were used as a basis to formulate and test the premise that, as group tasks become more equivocal or involve increasing levels of difficulty in achieving group consensus, social and contextual cues will have a greater impact on group interaction and on group and task outcomes.

Undergraduate psychology students were randomly assigned into 72 three-person same-sex groups. Each group worked on three tasks (idea generation, intellective, and decision making) either face-to-face or through a synchronous computer conferencing system. The order of tasks was completely counterbalanced.

Communication media had a substantial effect on the total and relative amounts of group communication. In contrast to face-to-face groups, computer-mediated groups engaged in far less total communication, had higher proportions of task to total communication, and expressed higher proportions of disagreement. Computer-mediated groups also showed more equal distribution of participation across group members than did face-to-face groups. In contrast to the findings reported by Kiesler and colleagues, computer-mediated groups did not express more negative interpersonal communication and had a higher proportion of positive interpersonal communication than did face-to-face groups.

Face-to-face groups were considerably more productive on all three tasks, and the interaction of task type and media affected task product quantity as expected. However, communication media had little effect on the quality of performance on the idea generation task. Computer-mediated groups were more dissatisfied with the process, and with their performance on the decision-making task. Computer-mediated groups also reported lower levels of interpersonal attraction.

Valacich, J., Dennis, A., & Connolly, T. (in press). Idea generation in computer-based groups: A new ending to an old story. *Organizational Behavior and Human Decision Processes*.

Previous research on brainstorming, an idea-generating technique, has generally found that interacting groups produce fewer ideas than do equivalent numbers of individuals working alone. Four experiments are reported that examined the effects of group size on the performance of groups using a computer-based idea generation system. The first three contrast groups of various sizes (3, 4, 6, 9, 12, and 18) to nominal groups of equal size. The results of these experiments were consistent; large groups (above nine members) using a computer-based idea generation system produced more nonredundant ideas than did equivalent nominal groups. Participant satisfaction increased slightly with group size. Average idea quality declined slightly with increasing group size for both EBS and nominal groups.

A fourth experiment sought to explain this finding. Participants were randomly assigned to nine-person groups and performed two separate idea generation tasks in a counterbalanced order. Half the groups (four groups) performed their tasks using the standard EBS procedure; the other half used a modified technology that allowed only one member to type ideas at a time. The standard EBS groups generated significantly more ideas, nearly four times more on average than the modified technology groups. The authors concluded that the elimination of production blocking in the computer-based groups accounted for a significant portion of the enhanced productivity of the computer-based groups.

Valacich, J. S., Dennis, A. R., & Nunamaker, J. F. (1991b). Group size and anonymity effects on computer-mediated idea generation. *Small Group Research, 23*(1), 49-73.

This experiment examined the effects of group size and group member anonymity on the performance of groups using a computer-mediated idea generation system. A 2 × 2 factorial design was used, crossing anonymity (anonymous or identified) with group size (three- or nine-member). Each of the four cells had between five and seven groups. The participants in the study were upper-division business students.

Large groups produced more nonredundant ideas, which therefore yielded higher total quality scores than small groups. Anonymity had no effect on idea generation, although identified groups were more satisfied and rated themselves somewhat more effective than anonymous groups. Members of small-identified groups made the fewest critical remarks, were the most satisfied and rated themselves more effective compared to group members in the other experimental conditions.

Valacich, J. S., Paranka, D., George, J. F., & Nunamaker, J. F. (in press). Communication concurrency and the new media: A new dimension for media richness. *Communication Research.*

An experiment investigated the effects of communication channel and proximity on the idea generation performance of groups. A 2 × 2 factorial design was used, crossing group member proximity (face-to-face vs. distributed) and communication channel (verbal vs. electronic). Five groups with five members were in each of the four experimental conditions. The participants were upper-division business students. The groups worked on an idea generation task.

Groups using electronic communication generated more ideas and better ideas than groups using verbal communication. Distributed groups did not significantly outperform face-to-face groups on any idea generation measures. Groups using verbal communication were not significantly more satisfied than groups using electronic communication, nor were groups in the face-to-face conditions significantly more satisfied than groups in the distributed conditions.

Vogel, D. R., & Nunamaker, J. (1988, September). Health service group use of automated planning support. *Administrative Radiology.*

A case study of a group in a health service organization reported high levels of satisfaction when using the Plexsys GDSS system for project planning. In addition, the participants found the system to be very effective. (No within-group or between-group comparisons were made.)

Walther, J. B., & Burgoon, J. K. (1992). Relational communication in computer-mediated interaction. *Human Communication Research, 19*(1), 50-88.

This study examined the effects of time and communication channel on relational communication (i.e., the messages that people use to define their interpersonal relationships) in groups. Prior research on the relational aspects of computer-mediated communication has suggested strong depersonalizing effects of the medium due to the absence of nonverbal cues. That research has been criticized for failing to incorporate temporal and developmental perspectives on information processing and relational development. The researchers describe and test an alternative—a social information-processing approach—to explain relational communication in computer-mediated groups.

Thirty-two three-person groups completed three decision-making tasks over a 5-week period. The participants were undergraduates at a large university. Half of the groups communicated face-to-face; the other half communicated through an asynchronous computer conferencing system. At the end of each task, group members completed 64 Likert-type items of a relational communication questionnaire.

Computer-mediated groups developed and evolved in relationally positive directions. Participants' ratings of one another's composure/relaxation, informality, receptivity/trust, and social (versus task) orientation became higher over time. The authors suggest that these findings imply that "cues-filtered-out" theories (e.g., Culnan & Markus, 1987) do not hold in, and the associated effects of greater task orientation, self-absorption, arousal, and impersonality do not occur in, extended-time, asynchronous computer interactions.

Watson, R., DeSanctis, G., & Poole, M. S. (1988). Using a GDSS to facilitate group consensus: Some intended and unintended consequences. *MIS Quarterly, 12,* 463-478.

This study investigated the effects of computer mediation and problem-solving structure on the level of group consensus for a task requiring resolution of conflicting personal preferences. Forty-four three-person and 38 four-person groups, composed of graduate and undergraduate students enrolled in introductory MIS classes, were randomly assigned to one of three experimental conditions: (a) a computer-based support system (GDSS), (b) a manual paper-and-pencil support system, or (c) a face-to-face condition without support. Each group worked on the "foundation task" that required groups to allocate a sum of money among competing projects that have requested funds from a philanthropic foundation.

The GDSS technology appeared to offer some advantage over no support, but little advantage over the manual, pencil-and-paper method of supporting group discussion. The average level of consensus improved and the variance in consensus was reduced following the group meeting for all three communication media conditions. A secondary analysis indicated that postmeeting consensus was positively related to premeeting consensus in the manual and GDSS groups only. The equality of influence among group members was not significantly different between the three conditions. There were no significant differences for group attitudes. Manually supported groups had the most positive attitudes toward group process. Groups using GDSS became very procedure oriented, rather than issue oriented, in their discussions.

Weisband, S. (1992). Group discussion and first advocacy effects in computer-mediated and face-to-face decision making groups. *Organizational Behavior and Human Decision Processes, 53,* 352-380.

This lab experiment examined the effects of communication media on the influence of the first person in a group to advocate a position. Possible explanations of the influence of a first advocate were tested in an experiment through these independent variables: (a) assignment of first advocate (self-selected/randomly assigned), (b) early discussion before advocacy (discussion/no discussion), and (c) mode of communication (face-to-face/electronic mail).

Twenty-four same-sex three-person groups participated in this study. Half of the groups were all female, the other half all male. The subjects were 72 Carnegie Mellon students: half undergraduate, half graduate. The design was a $2 \times 2 \times 2$ (Discussion × Assignment × Communication Mode) repeated measures in two blocks of Size 4. The two levels of discussion varied the timing of the first advocate's proposal (before or after group discussion). The two levels of assignment varied the way in which the first advocates proposed their solutions (self-selected vs. randomly assigned). The two levels of communication mode were face-to-face and computer-mediated group discussions. Each group was given instructions for coming to consensus on four choice dilemmas. Each choice dilemma involved a risky but attractive career alternative and a safer but less attractive career alternative.

The results provide strong evidence that initial group discussion—both face-to-face and electronic groups—positively affected first advocate's behavior. Several measures indicated that when groups began their interaction with a general discussion of the problem situation, the first advocate's proposal was closer to the final group decision than the average pregroup decision. With no early discussion, the proposal of the first advocate was closer to the average prediscussion preference than to the final group decision.

The content and tone of discussion in the computer-mediated group was clearly different from face-to-face discussions. Electronic discussions contained significantly more implicit preferences and explicit proposals, as well as more social pressure remarks, more uninhibited behavior, more task-irrelevant remarks, and proportionally fewer arguments, compared with face-to-face discussion.

Electronic groups also took more time to discuss a problem before someone advocated a position. However, the general process of group decision making seems to have been about the same. In both cases, people stated positions, group members generally stuck to the majority position, and with early discussion prior to advocacy, first advocates' choices predicted the decisions. In all cases, groups shifted toward an extreme position.

Zigurs, I., DeSanctis, G., & Billingsley, J. (1991). Adoption patterns and attitudinal development in computer-supported meetings: An exploratory study with SAMM. *Journal of Management Information Systems, 7*(4), 51-70.

This study explored the development of group attitudes in a group decision support system environment. Eight groups of four and five persons met in a computer-supported conference room (SAMM) and worked on two strategic planning tasks over a period of 2 months. Groups could decide whether to use the GDSS in each meeting. Members' attitudes toward group decision process and the quality of meeting outcomes were assessed after each meeting.

Groups did not necessarily move directly from novice to expert GDSS users, but seemed to follow a cycle of experimenting/learning/experimenting that took them through progressively more complex layers of the system. There were two patterns of group adoption of the GDSS technology: (a) groups that accepted the technology and used it throughout their meetings (adopters), and (b) groups that rejected the technology (discarders). The factors that contributed to adoption or rejection of a GDSS included resistance and inadequate learning by users, perceived mismatch of the technology with the task, real and perceived system inadequacies, and exogenous events.

Zigurs, I., Poole, M., & DeSanctis, G. (1988). A study of influence in computer-mediated group decision making. *MIS Quarterly, 12,* 625-644.

This study examined the effects of structure and computer support on the influence of members in groups. It tested a model of specific GDSS effects on influence behavior based on an information exchange view of decision making and on the impact of a GDSS as a communication channel.

Thirty-two three- and four-person groups worked on a task in which they had to choose a given number of individuals to be admitted to an international studies program from an applicant pool. The participants were undergraduate business majors enrolled in an introductory information systems course who chose their own group membership (project team) at the beginning of the school term. The majority of subjects were strangers to one another and selection was quasi-random. Groups were randomly assigned to experimental conditions. The independent variables included the type of technological support: computer-supported structured versus face-to-face manual (paper-and-pencil) versus unsupported face-to-face groups. The computer and face-to-face structured groups received the same group decision support features. Fourteen groups were in each of the two experimental conditions and four groups were in the unstructured face-to-face baseline conditions.

Influence behavior was measured by summing (a) verbal acts in five categories of Putnam's procedural coding system; (b) nonverbal procedural acts; and (c) group-messaging acts. The distribution of influence behavior was measured by calculating the within-group variance of average influence ratings that were assigned to individual group members by observers of the session videotapes. Performance was measured by the difference between subjects' predictions of applicants' success scores in the international studies program and the true success scores.

There were no significant differences between the overall amount of influence behavior attempted in computer-supported versus manual groups, although significant differences were found in the pattern of influence behaviors, that is, the different types of behaviors used. In addition, influence behavior was more evenly distributed among members in GDSS groups than in unsupported groups on one of two measures. Individual performance improved more in computer-supported groups than in manual groups and computer-supported groups performed better than manual groups in an absolute sense, although the differences were not significant. Qualitative analyses of how groups in the computer condition embraced the system showed that some accepted the system and used it advantageously, whereas others ignored the system's potential.

Author Index

Abel, M. J., 13, 14, 15, 126, 132
Adelman, L., 82, 126, 127, 144
Adrianson, L., 126
Aldag, R. J., 126
Allen, T. J., 126
Altman, I., 60-61, 133
Ancona, D. G., 28, 35, 50-51, 126, 127
Applegate, L., 138
Arendt, E., 133
Argote, L., 115, 127
Argyle, M., 127
Arrow, H., 62, 137
Arunachalam, V., 82, 127, 144
Atkins, D. E., 138

Baecker, R. M., 127
Barefoot, J., 127
Barfield, W., 127
Barley, S., 127
Baroudi, J., 134
Bastianutti, L. M., 82, 129, 131, 148, 149-150
Benjamin, R. I., 136
Berger, D. E., 132
Beswick, R., 127
Bikson, T. K., 4, 35, 46-47, 83, 115, 127, 128, 131, 132, 136, 148
Billingsley, J., 83, 143, 168-169
Blackwell, M., 128
Bobrow, D., 141

Bostrom, R. P., 83, 124, 128, 145
Bower, C., 135
Brobst, S. A., 136
Bui, T., 83, 128, 145
Bulick, S., 14, 126
Burgoon, M., 83, 143, 166-167
Burn, J. M., 128

Caldwell, D. E., 28, 127
Card, S. K., 138
Carley, K., 128
Carter, M., 138
Case, D., 140
Chaiken, S., 128
Chalfonte, B. L., 13, 14, 135
Champness, B. G., 128
Chapanis, A., 128, 143
Chidambaram, L., 83, 128, 145
Childress, W., 142
Christie, B., 53, 141
Cicourel, A., 128
Coffin, S., 14, 126
Cohen, M. D., 136
Connolly, T., 82, 83, 128, 134, 142, 146, 156, 165
Contractor, N., 57-58, 129, 140
Cooper, W. H., 82, 129, 131, 132, 149-150
Corey, D., 14, 126
Cornell, P., 138

Subject Index

175

About the Authors

Andrea B. Hollingshead joined the faculty of the University of Illinois, Urbana-Champaign, as Assistant Professor of Speech Communications in fall 1993. She received her Ph.D. in social psychology from the University of Illinois, Urbana-Champaign in 1993. Her current research interests include examining the effects of communication technologies on work groups and organizations and specifying the cognitive and social processes that lead to effective information pooling and processing in group decision making.

Joseph E. McGrath is Professor of Psychology at the University of Illinois, Urbana-Champaign. He received his Ph.D. in social psychology from the University of Michigan in 1955. His research interests include small group processes and performance, temporal and gender issues in social psychology, and research methodology.